Reaching for Immortality:
Can Science Cheat Death?

REACHING FOR IMMORTALITY: *Can Science Cheat Death?*

A Christian Response to Transhumanism

SANDRA J. GODDE

Foreword by Graham Joseph Hill

WIPF & STOCK · Eugene, Oregon

REACHING FOR IMMORTALITY: CAN SCIENCE CHEAT DEATH?
A Christian Response to Transhumanism

Wipf & Stock
An Imprint of Wipf and Stock Publishers
199 W. 8th Ave., Suite 3
Eugene, OR 97401

www.wipfandstock.com

PAPERBACK ISBN: 978-1-6667-3674-8
HARDCOVER ISBN: 978-1-6667-9550-9
EBOOK ISBN: 978-1-6667-9551-6

MARCH 8, 2022 10:25 AM

I dedicate this book to Joshua, Caleb, and Zoe,
my beloved progeny.

I also dedicate this message to the next generation of
believers who will carry the torch of the timeless gospel
and propel it into the future, extolling the majesty of the
Creator and his high purposes for humanity.

True religion brokers heaven to earth and brings eternity
to bear upon time and history. This is what we are called
to do in every generation, and especially when times are
uncertain, troubling, and rapidly changing. This message
is born from a passion to manifest the goodness of God
and to declare his involvement in history . . . not only in
this beautiful yet broken world, but also holding out the
glorious hope of the age to come.

Contents

Foreword

IN *REACHING FOR IMMORTALITY: Can Science Cheat Death?*, Sandra J. Godde asks crucial questions facing our age, which is dependent on science and technology and increasingly shaped by a transhumanist vision. What will it mean to be human in the future? Despite many misperceptions, Scripture has a high opinion of personhood, sexuality, human bodies, and the created order. As Christians, we need not fear the physical realm but rather celebrate the presence of God in our bodies and our world and embrace his renewing work within them. Human beings are created beings: formed by God in his image, profoundly relational, not self-sufficient. Our entire lives and futures are also a testimony to God's work of divine renewal and creative genius.

God meets us relationally, in our bodies and in our world, and transforms us by his grace and power. To be human is to be shaped by God from nothing and to be birthed into a process of being called and created, loved and desired. God lovingly invites us to glorify and witness to him in our bodies, in our world, and in history. Our bodies, sexualities, and world are a gift from God. We are continually being created and firmly located within the created order.

Although we are often deluded by visions of grandeur, self-sufficiency, or transcendence, we are not self-made. We are continually created out of the abundance of God's love and grace. We are formed by God and located within the world. So, we are interdependent, not merely sharing the origins of other created things but being woven by God into the fabric of the created order in mysterious and loving ways. Human sexuality and embodiment testify to God's presence in our lives and his love for our whole persons, including our bodies. We experience the love of God in our createdness and embodiment. God continually forms and sustains creation parentally. Human beings are a part of creation, enjoying the filial care and concern of the Creator.

We share the realities of gender, reproduction, sexual appetite, and sexual differentiation with other living creatures. Like other living things, these elements are subject to abuse, environmental factors, power and gender relationships, genetic influences, time and space, socialization, fear and intimidation, pleasure and free will, individuality, ambiguity, fluidity, and mystery. Our sexuality witnesses to our location within the created order and our reflection of the image of God. This sexuality mirrors the web of relationships that all created things share.

So, the dysfunctional urge to live as nonsexual, spiritual beings (I'm not referring to celibacy here), or, conversely, to indulge in self-serving, impersonal sexual practices are expressions of denial. Both deny the relational essence of our being and bodies. Both separate us from authentic intimacy and communion with the Other and with others. Both ends of the spectrum are dualistic, failing to recognize our relational embeddedness in the creation and God.

Our lives unfold in the theater of the body, world, and history. As created beings, the created order (or the "world") is the theater in which our lives unfold—sexuality, work, family, commitments, spirituality, politics, society, suffering, ecology, achievement, failure, the creative arts, and so on. Throughout history, the church's response to this location within the world and the body has been mixed, hostile, ambiguous, and, sometimes, gnostic. Religious and spiritual movements have moved between the poles of the deification of the sensual and the repulsion of all things unspiritual. They have sought to help believers escape the worldly realities of birth, death, sexuality, work, pain, and society. But this denies the biblical witness.

This world is in a real relationship with the divine, even though the Creator is clearly (and radically) distinct from it. Creation, including humanity, does not exist in autonomy from its Creator. Instead, we are recipients of God's ongoing creative processes, goodness, love, and presence. And so, humanity, as part of creation, gives glory to God. We are created to glorify God and enjoy intimate communion with God, others, and creation. This is our ultimate purpose. God does not neglect or disdain creation and bodiliness. Instead, creation (past, present, and future) is the place where God's glory is revealed and consummated.

As beings that are part of creation, we share the history of God's relationship with this world, along with the rest of creation. As creatures made in the image of God, we are uniquely charged with the care of creation. We are to treat the rest of creation with the honor that reflects how our identity and destiny are enmeshed with it and redeemed (by the person and work of Christ) along with creation. Human beings don't exist in a transcendent, subduing, monarchical relationship to the rest of creation. As part of creation, humanity participates, communes, communicates, loves, repents, and breathes in the mysterious interrelationships of the created order. We find salvation and divine life through the incarnational presence of God in this theater. Therefore, we must reject a dualistic, gnostic, dominating view of the world and creation. Human history attests to such a view as being destructive (i.e., nuclear proliferation, ecological destruction, unconscionable genetic experimentation, loss of biodiversity, global warming, and so on).

Our bodies are broken and dying. But they point to their Creator, and the redemption of our bodies and creation is our ultimate hope. This embodiment is in the world (we are immersed in structural and systemic realities—political, economic, social, religious, and the like). The theater upon which this drama is played is human history (time, space, matter, spirit, and body entwined in this cosmic drama since the world's creation). The body is animated and given form by the soul (the breath of God), and the soul expresses itself through the body. As a soul/body unity, we are located ontologically in the world. There is no other arena in which human beings "live and breathe and have their being" (Acts 17:28). We have this life in Christ and his world.

Grace presupposes and redeems human nature and bodiliness. Our bodies yearn for God (whether we recognize this or not). God infuses a broken, wounded, and conflicted world with hope for more through grace. God gives us hope and shalom through a biblical vision of bodily resurrection and the restoration of all creation to God and wholeness in Jesus Christ.

Reaching for Immortality: Can Science Cheat Death?, is no cloying attempt at a simplistic Christian approach to science, technology, or transhumanism. Sandra insists we do the hard work of engaging transhumanist visions, practices, and philosophies, while putting these into conversation with Christian biblical theologies of creation, personhood, human embodiment, ethics, and bodily resurrection. In *Reaching for Immortality: Can Science Cheat Death?*, Sandra equips Christians to examine and respond to the transhuman agenda regarding death and immortality, considering technological advances and biblical visions of the future. This book is an invaluable addition to any library of research into Christian responses to transhumanism.

GRAHAM JOSEPH HILL
Principal and Assoc. Professor of Global Christianity
Stirling College, Australia

Preface

MOST OF MY LIFE has been characterized by a quest for the divine. It has been a joyous but costly journey. As one who has pursued careers in both professional dance and theology, it seemed fitting for me to convey a message of wholeness and holiness, in both body and soul.

As a dancer, my body is my instrument; a beautiful and complex medium to express the artistry of one's soul, animated by the spirit within. Dancers carry a heightened understanding of the sacredness of their bodies to live in this world, and to express their craft with finesse. And yet, all human beings are fearfully and wonderfully made as a psychosomatic unity, and this is why doing away with the intricacies of the physical body (or making them *plastic*) disturbs me greatly. As a theologian, my orientation is to seek the divine in all facets of life; to understand who God is and the purpose for which we are made. It has been my calling and deep joy to share my passion for the disciplines of theology and dance with many students over multiple decades, and see their horizons expand in fruitfulness.

My own history has borne out this indivisible unity of body and soul in life experiences ranging from the euphoric to the tragic. I have witnessed the effects of the forces of good and evil on others' bodies and faces. I have also known the joyfulness of soulful embodiment in my dancing life and in the pursuit of the divine. I have felt the effects of sin, both my own and others, deep in my body, and recognized these consequences as a call for repentance and forgiveness.

I wanted to write a book that clearly expresses God's dream for humanity: for us to be immortalized in him, in a glorious union of body and soul, and live forever beyond death with a quality of life second to none. Though there are competing ideologies as to how this can be accomplished, I have chosen the way of loving fidelity and allegiance to Christ and his kingdom—an embodied spirituality.

My firm hope is that you, the reader, will likewise be inspired by the invitation of Christ to find true and everlasting life in him. This is the bliss we long for, the destiny for which we were fashioned.

Whom have I in heaven but You?
And besides You, I desire nothing on earth.
My flesh and my heart may fail,
But God is the strength of my heart and my portion forever.
(Ps 73:25–26)

Introduction

THE PIVOTAL QUESTION

Immortality is an ideal that humans have always dreamt of and longed for. The Christian gospel promises eternal life to those who believe and follow Christ; transhumanists, however, seek an ideal of their own making, one which is intrinsically bound with technology. In our reach for human progress and immortality, which pathway will lead to our future human flourishing? From ancient civilizations to the present, this inconsolable ache to live forever never wanes. Perhaps this is because "He (God) has also set eternity in their heart."[1]

The passion for this book was fueled by the singular question: Will cybernetic immortality ever trump the Christian hope of resurrection from the dead and the life of the world to come? In attempting to answer this question, the broader concept of what it means to be human, in light of the exponential technological growth envisaged for our future, needs to be explored. How important is embodiment for our personal identity? What is transhumanism and where is it leading us? How does the biblical understanding of personhood survive in a posthuman future?

At the forefront of science and ideology there converges a philosophical movement called transhumanism. Its proponents advocate a transformation of humanity by using advanced

---

1. Eccl 3:11.

1

technologies to enhance human intellectual capacities and upgrade our biology. Their goal is to overcome the human limitations of decay, suffering, and even death. Transhumanism is, simply put, man improving himself by merging with technology.

Great excitement surrounds the vision of the transhumanists as some seek to immortalize the mind by cheating death, and replace the natural body with a fabricated one, that is designed to be immune to death. But how far is too far with respect to some of these aspirations? While most would agree that goals such as developing cures for diseases, organ transplants, alleviating suffering, and developing prosthetics are good and uncontroversial, the goal to modify our human species into a technological hybrid is more controversial. Foremost futurist visionary Ray Kurzweil,[2] along with other proponents of the *Humanity+* movement, plan to do just that. Yuval Harrari also describes this as humanity's vision to become self-made gods in his book: *Homo Deus: A Brief History of Tomorrow.*[3]

Who doesn't want to live in a perfect world, where there is no death, aging, suffering, war, hardship, or conflict, and where there is a promise of eventual immortality? Christians believe the promise of a new creation is real. It is not just a utopian dream, but a destination with a guide and a known path. However, the transhumanists are a new breed of fellow travellers who also see a promised land. They too are confident that they will arrive in a utopian future. They also have a vision and a strategy, with technology as the path and development as the guide. Notwithstanding there are some core convergences between the transhumanist ideology and Christian orthodoxy in terms of aspirations, there are also some core divergencies at a fundamental level between these two worldviews. In particular, I would like to highlight from a biblical perspective how the body is part of the integrity and uniqueness of the human species, and should be preserved and dignified, not sought to be eradicated in the service of future progress for the human species.

2. Kurzweil, *Singularity Is Near*, 198–99.
3. Harrari, *Homo Deus*, 43.

Much of today's modern technology, such as genetic augmentation, cell regeneration, implantable devices that interact directly with the brain, artificial intelligence, robotics, cybernetics, nanotechnology, cloning, uploading the mind, and other technologies, point towards a transhuman future; that is, a belief that we are transitional humans on our way to becoming posthuman. Excitement surrounds the vision of the transhumanists as they hold out the ultimate prize of a technological immortality.[4] But can "cybernetic immortality"[5] realistically be achieved, and is it desirable for human flourishing, or consistent with faith in biblical redemption?[6]

Many argue we are already in a symbiotic relationship with technology with things like facial coding, wearables (like Apple watches and goggles), embeddables (chip implants), smart pills (ingested technology), replaceables (artificial eyes), designer babies (through genetic engineering and CRISPR-CAS technology), computer chips in brains, brain implants (your very own augmented mind), and other things. Scientists are also working on implantable memories and experiments have already been done in mice. There is also the concept of mind-uploading, and the "brain net," which is a form of virtual telepathy with every memory recorded and available on a cloud service. With these kinds of technologies developing at exponential speeds, many transhumanists say we are becoming a species that transcends and transforms our human biology into a posthuman state.

Posthumanism is the belief that eventually humans will develop enough, either technologically or biologically, to be able to transition themselves into beings that can no longer be considered simply human. Transhumanists talk about the technological singularity, and predict within fifteen years that the human species will develop superhuman machine intelligence that will change the fabric of what it means to be human. Some see this as a

---

4. Vicini and Brazal, "Longing for Transcendence," 148.

5. Both embodied Radical Life Extension (RLE) and disembodied cybernetic immortality (CI) are discussed in chapter 5.2.

6. Peters, "Radical Life Extension," 250.

technological imperative in a progressive evolution of the species, a human upgrade as it were. Some even say this is inevitable, that the genie is already out of the bottle, but what are the dangers involved in unfettered technology being unleashed upon our world, and what ethics will guide us in our future decisions?

We must pay attention to what lies on the horizon. For example, Elon Musk's new invention—Neuralink[7]—is a brain-machine interface (BMI) that promises to change everything. Not only can this device, inserted into the brain by a robot, fix anything wrong with the brain (hearing, eyesight, physical defects, lymph function, memory) but it can enable one to be connected to the internet of things truly making a full symbiosis between man and machine, increasing your brain capacity and allowing both input and output directly between brain and device. A lesser version of Neuralink is already being used for Parkinson's patients. If Musk's Neuralink discoveries advance, our future entails possibilities where technology will blur the distinction between our individual persons and machines. This in turn raises further ethical questions, not the least of which is: Who will control it all?

These are some of the questions that arise concerning the nature of the human person in the technological future:

1. Is this vision of some sort of superhuman or cybernetic immortality what we really long for as human beings?

2. Do these technological aspirations threaten what it is to be truly human and what we cherish the most about ourselves as human beings? Do we want to do away with all our vulnerabilities and weaknesses, including the capacity to love and to be wounded through our emotional and physical attachments, and our interdependence on all other living beings?

3. Are we merely biological machines that can upgrade or perfect ourselves through technology, or does our being "made in God's image" involve a more complex and satisfying teleological end, designed for us by a Living Creator? Namely,

7. Aperture, "Neuralink."

an end goal where communion with God and love for one another is the highest ethic and ultimate good.

4. What ought we seek to preserve and defend about our humanity, if anything, in the future, in light of these wild possibilities and exponential technologies?

5. In short: What is the best future for our human flourishing?

Furthermore, the most pressing concern of all is this: Do some of these technologies presently being hatched and envisaged for our future pose an existential threat to our future flourishing as human beings?

The Christian gospel offers us a very different end goal to the transhumanist's vision. It is a future where believers are resurrected from the dead in a corporeal body, thus the integrity of body and soul is preserved, and this underscores the centrality of the body for human beings bearing "*the image of God.*" While the posthuman agenda seeks to immortalize the mind by cheating death, the gospel offers something more than a promise of future, embodied immortality: It also addresses our current soul corruption now and resolves it comprehensively after death. While key transhumanists see death as a disease that must be overcome by technoscience, believers in Christ see death as a gateway into a greater metaphysical reality.

To replace the natural body with a fabricated one that is designed to be immune to death seems problematic on theological, philosophical, social, and ethical grounds. Both transhuman and posthuman agendas tap into our deepest desires and longings for immortality, revealing what means we would use to achieve those desires. What is the final goal of all our technological transformations? These agendas raise profound questions about what it means to be human, and what "technomoral virtues"[8] we need for the future.

In reaching for deification and immortality, will humanity grasp for eternal life by technological means, or receive it as a gift from the divine Creator? Will the posthuman agenda usher in

8. Vallor, *Technology and the Virtues*, 5.

an improved existence, or will it destroy what it is to be human? The aim of this book is to resource Christians to think deeply and respond to the transhuman agenda regarding death and immortality, in light of both developing technology and what Scripture reveals about the future.

OVERVIEW AND APPROACH

This book examines the anthropology of the transhumanists and their vision for immortality through technological means, and argues that our longing for human transformation is better fulfilled through the New Testament promise of resurrection in a corporeal body.

Chapter 1 will give a brief overview of transhumanist ideas and their influence in popular culture and place a broader context around the question of technological immortality. Chapter 2 will describe the main divergences between the transhumanist and Christian eschatologies; that is, the ultimate destiny of humanity. Three important components of Christian anthropology will then be compared with the transhumanist agenda. They are (i) the concept of the *imago Dei* (including creaturehood and deification), which will be addressed in chapter 3, (ii) the necessity of the body for complete personhood, which is the focus of chapter 4, and (iii) the centrality of the body in the eschatological hope of bodily resurrection, which is engaged in chapter 5. Chapter 6 will address some important ethical questions regarding proposed biological advancements concerning the human person and consider what aspects of human nature we ought to preserve and defend. Chapter 7 will offer some concluding thoughts.

The thesis of this book will argue that our physical body is essential to our humanity and personhood, and this contrasts sharply with the transhuman anthropology that "actively denigrates biological existence as negative and in need of technological transformation, whether in the form of bodily improvements, artificial bodies, or uploading consciousness."[9]

In human enhancement debates, theologians have concentrated on creaturehood. Following Burdett and Lorrimar,[10] I suggest that the concept of deification helps present a more robust theological anthropology: that the glorified body is granted incorruptibility in the reunion of soul and body; that personhood is recovered and renewed.[11] This affirms that *we are* our bodies.[12]

I also posit that true deification of human beings can only be initiated by divine grace. It is a gift of God that cannot be substituted by man-made technology. Conversely, a goal to deify our humanity, with no recognition of the impact of sin on our natures, or accountability to the God who created us, could be perilous and detrimental to society.

9. Thweatt-Bates, "Cyborg Christ," 1–2.

10. Burdett and Lorrimar, "Deification and Creaturehood," 247–50.

11. Labrecque, "Glorified Body," 166.

12. John Paul II, *Man and Woman*. Note that this is also affirmed widely in patristic writings.

Chapter 1

Transhumanism in Popular Culture

1.1 *TRANSHUMANISM IN FILM AND LITERATURE*

Many radical ideas from the transhumanist movement have made their way into popular culture, especially the movies. The power of visual media to explore controversial themes and to awaken the imagination of future possibilities is well understood. Transhuman ideas have exerted a deep influence on contemporary society and culture by endowing technology with a religious-like significance bordering on worship. Blockbusters like *The Matrix* (1999) and *Avatar* (2009) explore the themes of transcendence, alternative realities, parallel universes, and the possibility of a multiverse. These films often help blur the line between fact and fiction for their viewers.

The Matrix trilogy is deeply philosophical, raising fundamental questions about the nature of reality, humanity, and the choices that technology confronts us with. The Matrix movies emphasize the religious nature of transhumanism in the messianic hope of its main character, Neo. Traversing themes such as living within a digital simulation, to the potential dangers of artificial intelligence (AI), they raise questions not just of human technical prowess but of great spiritual portent. Other thought-provoking films include *Ghost in the Shell* (1995), *Lucy* (2014), *Expelled from Paradise (2014)*, *Advantageous* (2015), *Upgrade* (2018), *Replicas* (2018), *Anon (2018)*, *I Am Mother* (2019), *Code 8 (2019)*, and many others. These films explore themes around the nature of what it means to be human in an advanced technological world, the need for a biological body, the place of free will and memories in personhood, the value of human emotions and attachments, and that elusive part of humankind we often label "spirit" or "consciousness."

Transcendence (2014) depicts the full picture of transhumanism, and follows a scientist who is researching the nature of sentience as it relates to AI. As the plot unfolds, a group of Luddite terrorists poison him with polonium and this forces his supporters to upload his mind into his AI technology. This is a fictional representation of one type of cybernetic immortality that scientists are currently researching. The 2015 film *Ex Machina* is an emotional and ethical exploration of the dangers and potential of AI. It depicts a not-too-distant technology, and accentuates the far-reaching fears and chilling implications of robots going rogue.

Many movies center around the latest scientific technologies, advanced pharmaceuticals, genetic engineering, and cloning. *Splice* (2009) highlights the ethical implications of remixing genes, including creating human-animal hybrids. The plot-line explores the potentially dangerous and ethical consequences of refusing to destroy hybrid-human embryos being produced in research laboratories. Current real-life scientific practice ensures that such hybrids are destroyed before reaching a certain point of development, but what if that was not the case? Movies like *Limitless* (2014) explore the use of drugs to hypercharge one's brain so that it remembers every bit of information ever encountered, and this is in line with many neuroscientists' speculations of our brains' power of retention.

The modern classic *Gattaca* (1997) tells the story of a normal man born into a society where it is the norm to genetically engineer children to be superior, and depicts the horror of what it would be like to live in a genetic caste system. The movie *The Island* (2005) depicts a dystopian future where the central theme is cloning, and clones are kept in a regimented society to serve as organ donors for their real-life doubles. This film deals with the ethical problem of creating human beings purely for someone else's purposes.

RoboCop (1987 and 2014) deals with the theme of humans being given cybernetic bodies. In this instance the new body was given to allow the police officer to be the perfect blend of an unstoppable robot, and a thinking, emotional human. However, he was betrayed by those behind his regenesis who were only interested in having the perfect, submissive soldier, and he had to fight to maintain the last shreds of his humanity.

More recently there have been Netflix series such as *Black Mirror* and *Altered Carbon* that have dealt directly with cybernetic immortality. *Altered Carbon* (originally a novel by Richard Morgan) portrays a far-future world where immortality has been achieved by cybernetic means, and the human body has become just an interchangeable vehicle. The person or their brain/consciousness upload is called a "stack" and when they die they can be uploaded into another body, or "sleeve." The outcome, however, is very bleak; body-death becomes meaningless, and the gap between the megarich immortals and the expendable poor is widened exponentially. Humans, reaching to become gods, only corrupt their souls even more. Furthermore, the original creator of the technology used stages a violent uprising against the ruling elite in an attempt to undo the world she made, but fails.

These films question the nature of our human identity, our need for an actual biological human body, and the integrity of all the faculties of personal memory, free will, and emotions that constitute a person. However, if the essence of who we are is a transcendent and intangible soul, then how can AI mimic or recreate such a reality with wires and electrons?

These science fiction films give us a glimpse of what a world filled with AI and nanobots might look like. In popular culture there have also arisen many cyborg characters in television series such as the Cybermen in *Doctor Who*, or the Borg from *Star Trek*, Darth Vader from *Star Wars*, and "human" Cylons from *Battlestar*

Galactica. The enormously popular 1970s television series *The Six-Million Dollar Man* featured a bionic man who was a rebuilt astronaut, with superhuman strength, vision, and speed due to bionic implants. He was somewhat of a hero, employed by a secret agent of a United States government office, in the series that was based on Martin Caidin's 1972 novel, *Cyborg.*

However, cyborgs in fiction have often aroused a human contempt for an overdependence on technology, especially when it threatens free will or when the hybrids are used for war as military super-soldiers. As early as 1921, Czech playwright Karel Capek[1] premiered his science fiction play, *R.U.R.* (Rossum's Universal Robots) in Prague. The play explored the threat that modern technology posed to humanity in a dystopian plot that depicted a bleak vision where artificial life takes over the world, subsuming its creators. Mr. Rossum, the creator, typically representing the scientific materialist worldview, desired to create a chemical and biological artificial man, wishing to prove God unnecessary and obsolete. Capek states that he produced this play in order to draw attention to how modern mechanical technology can dehumanize us.

In 1932, Aldus Huxley[2] published his famous novel, *Brave New World,* wherein technology poses a threat to the very meaning of being human. The endgame here is bleak. The world is ruled by a small class of elites, driven by their own pleasures and ambitions. Reproduction is genetically controlled and monitored, and the masses are psychologically conditioned. The institutions of family, education, and religion are obliterated and there is no more personal autonomy. Human beings are mass produced, controlled, and treated like nothing more than machines. The problem with Huxley's dystopian future is that technology has empowered the privileged few to bring to fruition their illicit desires and selfish ambitions and has undone the significance and meaning of human life.

Each of the above literary classics portrays a disorientated humanity, crushed by the misuse of technology or the threat of

1. Capek, *R.U.R.*
2. Huxley, *Brave New World.*

technocratic elitism. Capek's fear is external, raising questions about survival when humanity loses control over technology. Huxley's fear is internal. His concerns are about human morality and are tied to human beings' propensity to indulge in their own selfish desires to the detriment of others. Neither author paints a picture of human flourishing. While continual technological advancement and progress can and does excite us with the expectation of pushing through new frontiers and enhancing our human experience, we would also do well to heed the potential pitfalls and addictive nature of this sort of power, especially when it lies in the hands of only a few imperfect human beings. Images from George Orwell's dystopian novel *1984* (1949) come to mind if we imagine a totalitarian world ruled by the omnipresent eyes of "Big Brother" through ubiquitous technology. The most portentous point of this novel is that it is possible that a future dictatorship or even multiple dictators could scrutinize every movement, word, and breath of a controlled population through the current technology of the internet of all things, resulting in a cruel, twisted world where human dignity and autonomy are belittled or abolished.

C. S. Lewis also warned about where we were heading with new technologies, coupled with increased government control, and spoke about this in his 1947 book *The Abolition of Man*. In it he said "what we call Man's power over Nature turns out to be power exercised by some men over other men with Nature as its instrument."[3] Lewis goes on to say "man's conquest of Nature, if the dreams of some scientific planners are realized, means the rule of a few hundreds of men over billions upon billions of men. There neither is nor can be any simple increase of power on Man's side. Each new power won by man is a power over man as well." In *That Hideous Strength* (1945), the third volume of his space trilogy, Lewis wrote about rogue science and unethical technocrats. He warned then that space travel could allow men to ignore sin and believe that technology would triumph over the universe. In that story the National Institute for Co-ordinated Experiments (N.I.C.E.) was a government bureaucracy established to help humankind,

3. Lewis, *Abolition of Man*, 35.

but did nothing of the sort. Using euphemisms and subterfuge as weapons of control, they "re-educated the maladjusted"[4] and cajoled the populace into submission to their plans. The physical sciences, good and innocent in themselves, were used in the service of mere power, deemed necessary for progress. This science fiction novel clearly reveals Lewis's deep concerns about unethical science and unconstrained technocracy. We would do well to heed his concerns.

1.2 WHY THESE QUESTIONS MATTER

Science and technology have changed our lives dramatically and they have the potential to improve the quality of our lives immeasurably. The vast improvements made in the field of medicine have increased life expectancy, reduced the rate of premature mortality, given us better hygiene and health, brought solutions to deadly diseases, and continue to conquer more and more physical and mental ills. Technology and computer science have improved the mechanization of increased productivity levels, made communication easier and faster, helped us to explore space extensively, and given us many other benefits. AI is also transforming our world by helping reduce human error, giving us digital assistance and faster decision-making capabilities, augmenting the work that humans do, storing and analyzing data on a monolithic scale, and improving efficieny in our workplaces. Technology and innovation are undoubtedly important, and scientific advances are exciting, however it is crucial that we are not blind to their negative effects on society as well. Machines have led to unemployment and environmental pollution. Science has put into our hands weapons of mass destruction like nuclear bombs, guided missiles, and the means of chemical and biological warfare. Moreover, unhealthy dependence on machines can deaden our sensibilities, stifle our creativity, enforce uniformity or boredom upon us and thus increase our wants and desires that tend to make us selfish, greedy, and cruel. Often

4. Lewis, *That Hideous Strength*, 45.

our moral and spiritual progress has lagged behind our scientific progress and we have allowed science to master us instead of using it as a servant for humanity. Rightly used, science and technology can bring a bit of heaven to earth; wrongly used, they can invoke hell by destroying our civilization.

The aspirations of transhumanists to merge humans with technology in increasing measure invokes controversial questions and differing views of human nature, namely, what it is, or what it could be. If one's view of human nature necessitates our biological connection to one another, to the natural world, to the food we eat, and to the natural systems we are a part of, we will not want to see human experience commodified and mechanized by a digitized world system.

Klaus Schwab (1938–), presently Chairman of the World Economic Forum (WEF), is a radical transhumanist. Along with Thierry Malleret, he wrote *COVID-19: The Great Reset*.[5] In this book the authors describe a narrative of how COVID-19 has disrupted our social and economic systems and what changes will be necessary to create a more sustainable world going forward. One is encouraged to radically rethink the nation state, the free market, capitalism, and individual freedoms in order to bring about this new world order. The plan entails a technological solutionism for our problems, chief of which are climate change, the coronavirus, individualism, and capitalism.

Schwab's transhumanism views are no secret. He speaks glowingly about "The Fourth Industrial Revolution,"[6] which is characterized by a slew of new technologies that fuse the physical, digital, and biological worlds. Combining humans and artificial intelligence, with an emphasis on nanotechnology and eugenics, the human being can be rewritten. Schwab says this future technology will impact all disciplines, economies, and industries, and will mean that we will face both great opportunities and great perils. The potential to connect billions of people to digital networks and significantly improve the efficiency of organizations may seem

5. Schwab and Malleret, *COVID-19*.
6. Schwab, *The Fourth Industrial Revolution*.

a very good idea, but what of the ability to intrude into private minds and read our thoughts and influence our behavior? Schwab speaks about the capacities of law enforcement agencies to use new techniques to determine the likelihood of criminal activity and perhaps even retrieve memories directly from people's brains to assess guilt. But is Schwab's vision a utopia of a brave new world, or is it more like a coercive dystopia? Are we being asked to trust self-appointed scientific experts with the future of our civilization, and what if their values are different from ours? Should we be pushing for more automation in the midst of a joblessness crisis, moving to normalize mass surveillance and biometric tracking tools, and allowing a singular power over global health policies? Without recourse to any conspiracy theory, the plain and observable fact is that there has been a transfer of wealth and power in the world since the COVID-19 pandemic, and there have been more prohibitive measures placed on ordinary people. Whereas 1 percent of the world's population owned 44 percent of wealth at the beginning of the pandemic, billionaires have now increased their wealth by more than 25 percent, while 150 million people have fallen back into extreme poverty.[7] Meanwhile trillions have been spent to bail out multinationals and backstop markets, and pandemic profiteering is rampant. The accepted and observable power of some international corporate entities cannot be denied. We can observe the economic movement and the types of decisions being made by our governments and politicians, without speculating on whether there is a shadowy cabal behind it all. Censorship is being done by government officials in league with internet titans.

Meanwhile, Mark Zuckerberg strides onto the world scene to inspire us about the next phase in technology interconnectivity and the new "Metaverse."[8] Zuckerberg imagines the next platform that will allow us to connect in an even more immersive way than texts, phones, and videos, and seeks help concerning how we can

7. "World Inequality Report 2022." See also John, "Pandemic Boosts Super-Rich Share of Global Wealth"; Neate, "Billionaires' Wealth Rises"; Peterson-Withorn, "How Much Money."

8. Zuckerberg, "Connect 2021."

all do this together. He speaks glowingly of an "embodied internet"[9] where one can experience life virtually, and this is the *Metaverse*. In this vision of the future all things we do online will be made "more natural and vivid,"[10] as screens alone cannot convey all the facial features and the full range of human connection we crave. You can do almost anything you can imagine: work, learn, play, shop, create, and attend family gatherings, as well as entirely new categories of activities which are still to come. Zuckerberg says that the present internet "cannot deliver that deep feeling of presence,"[11] but the next version of the internet can. However, the question arises: Why wouldn't we want to continue to enjoy personal, face-to-face interactions, local community involvement, tactile hugs and kisses from loved ones, and only leave technology to bridge the gaps of interaction when the personal touch is not possible? Do we really want technological advances to take over our embodied lives as human beings? What of the tactile, embodied existence of tasting good cuisine, smelling the scent of roses, touching the skin of a loved one, feeling the wind in one's hair, and standing on the seashore? Do we want to outsource our internal reality to Facebook/Meta?

Zuckerberg concedes that his metaverse does not yet fully exist, however the building blocks are in place. He seeks to awaken an excitement in others to join him in this ambitious goal for the future. Unpacking the vision, he invites one to imagine a world of socializing in the metaverse, where you put on your glasses or headset and you are instantly in your home space and then can connect with others. The defining quality of the metaverse is "the feeling of presence,"[12] that is, that you really feel like you are physically there with other people. We represent ourselves as avatars in this medium; a living, three-dimensional representation of you! You can design your own home space, invite people over, play games, create a home office, and teleport to anywhere you want to

---

9. Zuckerberg, "Connect 2021," 1:12.
10. Zuckerberg, "Connect 2021," 2:47.
11. Zuckerberg, "Connect 2021," 3:00–3:01.
12. Zuckerberg, "Connect 2021," 6:13.

go by clicking a link. While this does sound fun, does it make our lives better? Does disconnecting from the real world and living in an artificial construct help us to connect to reality, or abstract us from our inner reality? What good would it be if the temptation to escape into a fantasy world online was overwhelming, causing one to avoid real-life people and challenges, and possibly even neglecting to feed or care for one's children, for example?

Zuckerberg states that new forms of governance and eco-system building will be required for the metaverse and assures us that privacy and safety concerns will be addressed, allowing one to block unwanted people or teleport yourself to your own bubble to be alone if you so desire. Physical devices like screens will become unnecessary as holograms will take their place. One will be able to bring things from the physical world into the metaverse. This includes any type of media that can be digitized, like photos, movies, art, books, music, and games. You will be able to move across the different experiences through a choice of devices, including virtual reality (the immersive experience), augmented reality (through glasses), or through a computer or phone. Furthermore, there will be new ways of interacting with devices. Instead of typing, one can use gestures, words, or even thoughts. Zuckerberg states that a lot of this will be mainstream in five to ten years.

Horizon is the basic social platform to interact in the meta-verse. Horizon Home will include a social version where one can invite their friends to watch movies together; Horizon Worlds will allow one to build their own worlds and invite others to join; and Horizon Workrooms is created for collaboration. Beyond this, Zuckerberg unpacks what will be possible in the entertainment and gaming realms. One must visually see his presentation to glimpse the possibilities and potentialities of future technology. You will be able to join your friend overseas at a music concert, or have a far more immersive gaming experience, or engage in fitness pro-grams, working out in new worlds. Better tools for remote working conditions or hybrid working environments are being created for working in the metaverse. Education and learning in the meta-verse will be dramatically enhanced by implementing immersive learning content. Put on a headset or goggles and teleport yourself to places in history, or into outer space, or learn how to do guided surgery. Horizon Marketplace will also allow people to buy and sell both digital and physical products online. However, many creators and developers are needed to build all the infrastructure for these brave new initiatives.

Many of these visionary goals for the next decade are exciting and extraordinary, but there are challenges and uncertainties involved with such bold new advances. Although one can praise the ingenuity of such powerful tools, are these initiatives what we really need in this current climate? Zuckerberg is quick to emphasize that the metaverse will be built responsibly, taking into consideration the ethical principles of safety, privacy, transparency, and the consideration of all interests. Best practices have been sought through independent research and grants, and input has been invited from a wide variety of experts. The next frontier is the metaverse; the iconic social media brand of Facebook is morphing into a new company brand of "Meta," which will encompass the full breadth of what the company is presently doing and the future they want to build. This future will be built in collaboration with creators, developers, and other businesses in order to create a more open platform and a bigger, more creative economy. Welcome to the Metaverse: the internet of the future! This envisaged future is where you can put on a pair of glasses and step beyond the physical world into the kinds of experiences that one can only imagine. These inventions are not in and of themselves positive or negative. The question is: To what use will they be employed, and what ethics will guide them? What one can potentially do with a system like this could be terrifying. Furthermore, will technology of this scope, scale, and potential be another nail in the coffin of true, embodied humanity?

As we move into the next phase of humanity the questions surrounding what it is to be truly human are bound to be the types of questions we as a society will have to face. However, in exploring and imaging a future of human flourishing for ourselves, one must admit the extent to which our advances in technology have formed and are forming us as human beings.[13] Do we want to primarily live in a virtual-reality future, or do we want to maintain our embodied existence and prioritize our flesh-and-blood relationships and physical experiences? How can the message of the Christian gospel and its traditions evaluate the present culture and its social changes in regards to issues of human well-being and justice, since "the Church has always had the duty of scrutinizing the signs of the times and of interpreting them in the light of the Gospel?"[14]

While theologians can appreciate and applaud the beneficial uses of technologies to enhance human experience, they may also recognize that some of the proposed solutions to ease the world's malaise, or to improve the world, may over the long haul be worse than the natural problems themselves although they appear as a noble pursuit to benefit humankind.[15] This book will now turn to the key issue it was intended to address: that is, to highlight the important distinction between striving for the *homo cyberneticus* (human-AI integration) and the *imago Dei* (image of God). It will emphasize how the body is an integral part of the uniqueness of being human from a biblical and theological perspective, and argue that it should be dignified, not sought to be eradicated or superseded by technology.

13. Shatzer, *Transhumanism and the Image of God*, 9.

14. Vatican Council II, "Church in the Modern World," para. 4.

15. Hollinger, "Biotechnologies and Human Nature," 187.

CHAPTER 2

Convergences and Divergences between Transhumanist and Christian Views of Immortality

2.1 THE ESCHATOLOGY OF THE TRANSHUMANIST

Transhumanism is a philosophical orientation towards "techno-logical solutionism"[1] and is generally undergirded by a belief that radical technological progress will eventually disrupt society and redefine the very definition of the human being. A widespread notion in transhuman ideology is the anticipation of a future event called "the singularity." This culminating event will happen when the capabilities of humans will be assumed by either a super artificial intelligence or a hybrid of humankind and machines. In this scenario, human beings will have transformed themselves into transhumans who have freed themselves from the physicality of their bodies and have thus cheated death. The leading theorist of this technological singularity is Ray Kurzweil, a futurist who estimates its occurrence between 2040 and 2045. According to

1. Throughout his book, *To Save Everything, Click Here,* Evgeny Morozov used this term to describe the gurus of Silicon Valley.

CONVERGENCES AND DIVERGENCES

Kurzweil, it will be possible to reverse-engineer the human brain, emulating it on dry hardware, along with the whole spectrum of human emotions, thus mastering it and subsequently uploading the entire pattern of a human brain to a machine or synthetic body. This, it is argued, will result in the possibility of humans being severed from their "wet, biological component" so that their consciousness will go on forever, provided backup copies are created in case the hardware is destroyed.[2] Kurzweil sees this as a technological imperative in a progressive evolution of the species; a "human upgrade" as it were.[3]

In 2008, Sandberg and Bostrom analyzed the different possibilities of achieving a complete emulation of the human brain.[4] They distinguished "simulation" (imitating system output) from "emulation" (imitating internal causal dynamics), and stated that successful human brain emulation would require the same output behavior as the original brain, albeit at a faster speed. These ideas fueled the European Commission-funded Human Brain Project, whose goal was to achieve an emulation of the human brain on a computer.[5] Established in 2013 to research neurological diseases, this research was expected to pave the way for a self-conscious artificial intelligence. However, many criticisms have delayed this project to beyond its 2023 target.[6]

This futuristic vision where AI reigns is already the theme of many movies and novels. The idea of a person's consciousness being saved on a disk and then uploaded to other "bodies" (called "sleeves") after death, is the theme of Richard Morgan's science fiction novel *Altered Carbon* (2002, now a Netflix series). In the narrative, religious believers refuse the mind-uploading and therefore die permanently. Robin Hanson, who is the economist at Future of Humanity Institute, also explored what a future would look like if emulations ruled in his book *The Age of Em: Work, Love and Life*

2. Paura, "Rapture of the Nerds?," 343–67.
3. Kurzweil, *Singularity Is Near*, 198–99.
4. Sandberg and Bostrom, "Whole Brain Emulation."
5. Paura, "Rapture of the Nerds?," 352–53.
6. Paura, "Rapture of the Nerds?," 353.

When Robots Rule the Earth. Ems are AIs derived from an emulation of the human brain which humans can assign work tasks to in order to free themselves for other activities. Some *ems* would have robotic bodies, but some would live in virtual worlds. In this future, human beings as we know them might not exist at all, or if they do, will be a rare species. The ems would take over as the next step in evolution, replacing us and becoming the dominant race on our planet.[7]

Max Tegmark defines this new hybridization of human and artificial intelligence as *life 3.0*.[8] He speaks glowingly of the idea that emulations represent our "future descendants"[9] as he sees them as more capable of solving the upcoming challenges. In his book, *Life 3.0*, he cites futurist Hans Moravec, in his seminal book *Mind Children* (1988), as saying "we humans will benefit for a time from their [intelligent emulations] labors, but sooner or later, like natural children, they will seek their own fortunes while we, their aged parents, silently fade away."[10] Tegmark also remarks that it is possible to foresee the human species disappearing altogether. This could be achieved by either the AIs violently destroying our species, or by the human race being extinguished before developing AIs to this extent.

Many of these ideas have been influenced by Tipler's Omega Point theory.[11] The Omega Point theory is the belief that everything in the universe is destined to spiral towards a final point of unification; a future where life in any form will exist and live forever. Tipler identifies this Omega Point singularity, where infinite informational capacity is achieved, as God. The term was originally coined by Pierre Teilhard de Chardin (1881–1955), a French Jesuit priest, who stated that the Omega Point resembled

---

7. Hanson, *Age of Em.*

8. Tegmark, *Life 3.0*.

9. Tegmark, *Life 3.0*, 238.

10. Tegmark, *Life 3.0*, 239.

11. Tipler, *Physics of Immortality*, 483–88. See also Tipler, "Omega Point as Eschaton," 217–53.

the *logos* in Scripture: Christ, who draws all things unto himself.[12] The idea was developed further by Frank Tipler, a professor of physics and mathematics, in 1994. In Tipler's theory the universe is closed and will eventually collapse back in a very specific way into a final pointlike singularity. The Omega Point theory is based on a premise of Von Neumann's cellular automata that holds that consciousness can be replicated computationally: that is, the belief that the laws of life can be replicated on a computer and evolve from a simple level to a self-conscious complexity.[13] Therefore the spread of intelligence into the future can be achieved through self-replicating machines that will colonize various planets and eventually fill the entire universe. However, this cybernetic evolution of our species depends upon the premise that life is identified with information alone. The question arises: Isn't life more than just information, preserved and produced eternally? What about the animating force that drives all living organisms?

Yuval Noah Harari[14] distinguishes two types of transhumanist ideologies—one being "techno-humanism" and the other "dataism." Both are based on the premise that human volition is compromised or disappears once authority transfers from human beings to algorithms. While techno-humanism advocates using technology to enhance humans and achieve an updated version of a human being (the *Homo Deus*), dataism is a different concept. It is based on the understanding that the laws concerning data flows operate the same in both biochemical and electronic algorithms. Underlying this belief is the claim that the human being cannot be distinguished from the cellular automata.

Therefore, some transhumanists argue that once human intelligence is entrusted to programmed algorithms which are able to learn autonomously (machine learning), they would be far superior to humans for increasing data processing and should therefore replace them. The result: *Homo sapiens will become*

---

12. Teilhard de Chardin, *Science and Christ*.

13. Von Neumann and Burks, *Theory of Self-Reproducing Automata*.

14. Harari, *Homo Deus*, 367.

extinct.[15] Such is the eschatology on the far end of the continuum of transhumanists.

Transhumanists are not all secularists: some have sought a bridge to unite religious beliefs with transhumanist ideologies. One such organization is the Mormon Transhumanist Association (MTA), founded in 2006, which joined the World Transhumanist Association (now called *Humanity+*). The MTA believes that the search to exalt ourselves by scientific knowledge and technology is ordained by God. They further claim the possibility that God may even be an advanced man-machine hybrid. The Christian Transhumanist Association (CTA) was formed and affiliated with *Humanity+* in 2014. The CTA claim that God's mission of transforming and renewing all of creation can be done by using science and technology, albeit in an ethical manner. They also draw upon Teilhard de Chardin as a forerunner for their movement and recommend Tipler's *The Physics of Immortality* as a text to help understand the connection between Christianity and transhumanism.[16]

Another notable organization is the Turing Church, founded by Giulio Prisco (former Director of *Humanity+*). Inspired by Russian "cosmism" (initiated by the philosopher Nikolaj Fedorovic Fedorov),[17] Prisco argues that resurrection of bodies can be achieved by bringing back atoms of those who have died in the past and reconfiguring them as they were prior to death. He states that our reality may be analogous to a computer simulation and that God may be the super-programmer.[18] He also posits that the afterlife may also be a simulation or perhaps we wake up in the real world after death. It is clear from the notable examples above that the transhumanist's ideologies are ambitious, seemingly fixated on using technology to immortalize the human in one way or another. Life extension is their technological substitute for eternal life.

15. Harari, *Homo Deus*, 367.
16. Paura, "Rapture of the Nerds?," 356.
17. Young, *Russian Cosmists*.
18. Prisco, "Christianity and Transhumanism Are Much Closer."

2.2 THE ESCHATOLOGY OF THE CHRISTIAN: A COMPARISON WITH TRANSHUMANISM

The first and critical difference between Christian eschatology and transhumanism is the nature of the human being. The transhumanist goal of a self-directed evolution where humans are paramount in their own development and destiny contrasts with the Christian notion that human beings already possess a precise telos, designed and willed by God, and undergirded by the doctrine of the *imago Dei*. This concept of human beings being made "in the image of God" (derived from Gen 1:27), with a design and God-given purpose, presents a challenge to transhumanist ideologies.

The biblical concept of the *imago Dei* must be distinguished from the mind/body dualism of the Greeks and agnostics. Biblical theology maintains the mind-body entirety as being in the image of God and that this image is stamped all over the sphere of human corporeality. This is expressed both in the doctrine of incarnation (where God represents himself in corporeality through Jesus Christ) and in the doctrine of the resurrection (where Christ is raised in a human, glorified, bodily form).[19] The goal in Christianity is not to be rid of the frail and mortal physical body but to have the body redeemed and resurrected in a new form. Furthermore, the International Theological Commission states that human beings do not have rights to dispose of their own body because humans are not objects but "ends in themselves." Therefore, "given that man (sic) was also created in God's image in his bodiliness, he has no right of full disposal of his own biological nature. God himself and the being created in his image cannot be the object of arbitrary human action."[20] Also, the Christian understanding of sin is not derived from the dualistic contrasts of spirit and body, or reason and matter, but rather is a deliberate turning away from God and his ways, of which suffering is a consequence.

19. Simut, "Doctrine of the Resurrection of the Body," 31–45.

20. International Theological Commission, "Communion and Stewardship," 81–84.

Biblical theology is woven together with three themes: a good creation, the fall or corruption of creation, and the redemption of all things. Scripture states that all created reality came from God and was originally and intrinsically good, and that human beings were created as stewards of the physical earth and accountable to their Creator. When humanity sinned, the created order became marred and corrupted. At the very end of this age, God will redeem and restore creation, eliminating sin as an alien force and creating new heavens and a new earth.[21] As humanity's and creation's destiny are bound together,[22] the entire physical creation will be transformed, with believers being saved together with the material world, not out of it. The new earth will not be a negation of the physical world but an enhancement, purification, and glorification of this life, of which Jesus's resurrection is a foretaste. In this *new created order*, believers will live in renewed bodies, without corruption or sin.[23] The gospel is neither body-denying nor body-indulging, but offers a truly incarnational mode of being, where divine life is infused through the human person and eternal life is promised after death.

Although Philip Hefner[24] states that God created humans as *co-creators* to participate in creation in an active way, an argument that this extends to, or justifies overcoming or altering our biological limits as part of God's design for us, seems to hint at hubris and contradicts the doctrine of the *imago Dei*. If humans were created in the image of God, *Homo sapiens* represent God's ambassadors on earth and should not be considered further perfectable in essence, notwithstanding their corruption due to the entrance of sin. For Christians, the problem in humanity is the presence of sin, not corporeality and its limitations. Furthermore, Christ validated the good design of humanity when he incarnated himself in a human body that was not enhanced in any way.

21. Pearcey, *Love Thy Body*, 45.

22. Romans 8:21 states "the creation itself will be liberated from its bondage to decay and brought into the freedom and glory of the children of God."

23. Pearcey, *Love Thy Body*, 38–39.

24. Hefner, "Evolution of the Created Co-Creator," 512–25.

Christianity is about human transformation, but not in the way that technological solutionists propose. Christ came to deal with human sin and its consequences, and to give his life in atonement to abolish the power of death and sin.[25] Accepting that Christ's sacrifice is made for us means humans can be born anew into his kingdom of righteousness, experience forgiveness for their sins, begin a transformation of their moral nature through the sanctifying work of the Holy Spirit, and eventually be resurrected to eternal life after death.[26]

Both Christianity and transhumanism aspire to Godlike powers and perfection for human beings, but Christianity maintains that this cannot be achieved apart from the grace of God.[27] This Christian claim of deification is often expressed with reference to Irenaeus: "if the Word has been made man, it is so that men may be made gods."[28] This has shaped Christian thought through Athanasius, Gregory of Nazianzus, Gregory of Nyssa, and many Church fathers and orthodox theologians. God, through Christ, made the descent to the ultimate limit of humanity's fallen condition, including death, to open up a path of ascension for the union of human beings with divinity.[29] Human enhancement and immortality through technology is a very different pathway to perfection and fulfillment than the way of Christianity—one leaves God out of the equation, while the other has God's actions as instrumental. One denies the importance of the human body, the other affirms embodiment as central.[30]

The divergences between these two worldviews is underlined when one considers "the eschatological concept of a future technological singularity that would guarantee immortality in a sort of

25. Romans 6:23 states "for the wages of sin is death, but the gift of God is eternal life in Christ Jesus our Lord."

26. Heb 9:11–12; John 3:7; 1 Pet 1:23; Matt 26:28; Acts 2:38; 10:43; 26:18; Eph 1:7; Col 1:14.

27. Eph 2:8–9; Rom 4:6.

28. Irenaeus, *Against Heresies*, bk 4, ch. XXXVIII.

29. Rom 5:15; 6:8; 7:4; 8:34; 14:9.

30. Cole-Turner, *Transhumanism and Transcendence*, 5–6.

simulation at the end of time, as in Tipler's theory."[31] In Christian theology, immortality cannot be achieved without death.[32] The *Catechism of the Catholic Church* states: "to rise with Christ, we must die with Christ: we must 'be away from the body and at home with the Lord.' In that 'departure' which is death the soul is separated from the body. It will be reunited with the body on the day of resurrection of the dead."[33]

The Christian doctrine of the resurrection entails eternal life residing in a physical body, with the soul reuniting with its transfigured body, not merely a ghostly form. Christ's own resurrection was the firstfruits of many other believers who will join him in an imperishable body at a future time.[34] Jesus said "see my hands and my feet, that it is I myself; touch me and see, for a spirit does not have flesh and bones as you see that I have."[35] Thomas Aquinas maintained that the human person is an inseparable unity of body and soul. Although at death the soul is separated and the body perishes, the soul retains its inclination to be reunited with its body. While the body is dead, the soul continues to exist precisely because this separation is only temporary.[36] Underlying this doctrine is the idea that the mortal body is not a cumbersome host to be disposed of in order to achieve perfection and divinity, but rather is to be seen as the "temple of the Holy Spirit."[37]

In contrast to this glorious resurrection of the body and person as a unit, the transhumanists view the human body as a disposable commodity to be overcome and discarded. Their vision of the future sees the mind-uploading of a person as an intermediate step where the fragile physical body is disposed of. Their eventual

31. Paura, "Rapture of the Nerds?," 358.

32. Two possible biblical exceptions are Enoch and Elijah (Gen 5:22–24; 2 Kgs 2:11).

33. *Catechism of the Catholic Church*, 1005.

34. Matt 22:31; John 5:25; Acts 17:32; 23:6; 1 Cor 15:12, 20, 21, 42; Rev 20:3–5.

35. Luke 24:39. See also Luke 20:36; John 5:29; 11:25.

36. Aquinas, *Summa Theologiae*, I, Q.75, A.4.

37. 1 Cor 6:19.

goal is for the disembodied consciousness to be reincarnated into a new, perfect, and immortal body, created by humanity. The eschatology of the transhumanist that posits a posthuman entity dislodged from its biological body is vastly different than the biblical eschatology of eternity of the entire human person. These different visions for the future of humanity yield mutually exclusive endgoals for human flourishing.

CHAPTER 3

Limitations of Our Creaturehood

3.1 BENEFITS AND CONSTRAINTS OF HUMAN CREATUREHOOD AND FINITUDE

Many theological scholars have maintained that our creaturehood, endowed by God, plays a central role in adjudicating the desired limits of applying enhancement technologies to the human person.[1] They have extolled the benefits of our creaturehood and the virtues of our embodiment. Being a creature involves dependence, contingency, and limited capabilities. Should we seek to overcome this delineated scope of power God granted us? Is our circumscribed dominion on the earth a curse or a blessing?

The benefits of human limitation have been argued in recent times by a number of different Christian thinkers. Deane-Drummond argues that human enhancement goals mitigate against the joys of bodily life as a creature, seeing them as weaknesses and obstacles to overcome.[2] Thweatt-Bates champions the inherent good in many human-embodied experiences, with a focus on

---

1. Burdett and Lorrimar, "Deification and Creaturehood," 247.

2. See Deane-Drummond, "Taking Leave of the Animal?," 115. See also Deane-Drummond, "Remaking Human Nature."

the disabled.[3] Burdett maintains that virtues such as mercy, love, humility, and grace are only formed in community, where interdependence upon one another is required to overcome limitations and weaknesses.[4] Waters and McKenny both emphasize that human limitations are germane to creaturehood and necessary for genuine relationships and human flourishing. Waters further states that birth and death are essential features of our creaturehood and therefore should be dignified. He believes our contingency yields a good far outweighing the advantages proposed by the transhumanists of an extended life.[5] McKenny argues that the ultimate good for humanity can only be achieved through divine grace, not by technological means.[6] I will argue, along with many theological voices, that our creaturely humiliation and interdependence plays a crucial role in what it means to be human, and in upholding our dignity.

According to transhumanism, our body is the main problem, imposing what they consider to be intolerable restrictions upon what we can achieve and what we aspire to be. For example, the body constrains the will and we are limited by its frailty. As an embodied human being we suffer pain and are vulnerable to injury and sickness. We grow old and die. According to a transhumanist ideology, we must wage a technological and medical war against aging and death in order to save ourselves from our finite and mortal bodies. Max More, a leading transhumanist, says "aging and death victimize all humans placing an unacceptable imposition on the human race, therefore the technological conquest of aging and death stands out as the most urgent, vital, worthy quest of our time."[7] The methods heralded to do so include advances in genetic engineering, biotechnology, nanotechnology, computer

---

3. Thweatt-Bates, *Cyborg Selves*, 152.

4. Burdett, *Eschatology and the Technological Future*, 238.

5. Waters, "Whose Salvation? Which Eschatology?," 172. See also Waters, "Flesh Made Data."

6. McKenny, "Transcendence, Technological Enhancement, and Christian Theology," 185.

7. More, cited in Waters, "Whose Salvation? Which Eschatology?," 165.

science, bionics, and regenerative medicine. Age can be slowed down, physical and cognitive performance can be enhanced, and lives can be extended. These advances stem from the view that *Homo sapiens'* bodies are poor hosts for the intelligence that resides in their souls, and technological development can be used to escape the restraints that nature has imposed upon us. If dying can be a choice rather than a necessity then humans can be saved from their bodies and death is defeated. The rhetoric of the transhumanist goes: through technology we can transform ourselves into a superior, even immortal, posthuman species, and for many this becomes a moral responsibility, not just a technological possibility.[8]

Just how do the transhumanists propose to achieve immortality? Their strategy can be seen in three different approaches. The first is *biological immortality*. In this approach, championed by Aubrey de Grey, anticipated genetic and biotechnologies will be able to deal with degenerative mutations and defects and genetically boost immune systems.[9] The second method is *bionic immortality*. With advances in robotics and nanotechnology, body parts can be replaced with artificial substitutes like synthetic blood vessels or skin, or prosthetics. Neuroenhancers can be inserted into the brain to prevent loss of memory or cognitive function, and nanobots can be injected to replace or repair diseased organs. In theory, a bionic being could live forever, however there are many liabilities and restraints on such a being, such as malfunctions. This hybrid host is still vulnerable to accidents and death. The final and most controversial approach is *virtual immortality*. Ray Kurzweil and Hans Moravec, leaders in the fields of robotics and artificial intelligence, argue that information contained in a person's brain, including memories, experiences, and personality, can be digitized and then scanned and uploaded into a computer.[10] Once this operation is complete the information can then be downloaded into a robot or a virtual reality host. In doing so, one's virtual self could

8. Waters, "Whose Salvation? Which Eschatology?," 165–66.

9. De Grey, "War on Aging."

10. Kurzweil, *Age of Spiritual Machines*. See also Moravec, *Mind Children*.

remain immortal by updating it with backups, and the uploading and downloading process could be repeated indefinitely.[11]

When the argument is raised that human persons cannot be reduced to algorithms or digital patterns, Kurzweil and Moravec respond that the mind is ultimately who and what a person is, and as the mind is not a material object it is essentially information.[12] Furthermore, a biological body is only a natural prosthetic that hosts these information patterns. The goal is to liberate the mind from the biological body, because, as Moravec says, "I am preserved, the rest is mere jelly."[13] Such a view sees embodiment as an enemy to be overcome rather than a defining, and arguably glorious, feature of a being bearing the *imago Dei*. In contrast to this, a Christian view holds that our finiteness and mortality reminds us we are only creatures, created by a Creator, and we are not self-made. Although a Christian does not maintain that finitude, mortality, suffering ,and death are inherently good, it is a sober reminder that we, as a race, have fallen from the glory we once had at our creation by a good God. In death, Christians hold to the hope of a resurrected body, one which is both the same as that allotted to at birth, and yet infinitely superior in function and glory, without the corruption of sin.[14]

The vision of the transhumanists holds that humans should be saved from their finitude and mortality through a superior posthuman species. Waters states that Christian theology cannot embrace this strategy for similar reasons to why it rejected the Manichean and Pelagian heresies in the past.[15] Transhumanism echoes the same Manichean disdain for the body as corrupt or evil and from which the soul must be liberated, this time attempting to negate the body altogether by technology. Similarly, we see the Pelagian heresy reemerge with the reiteration of the force of

---

11. Waters, "Whose Salvation? Which Eschatology?," 167.

12. Waters, "Whose Salvation? Which Eschatology?," 167.

13. Moravec, *Mind Children*, 117.

14. Rom 6:3–7; 7:24, 8:11–13; 1 Cor 15:42–44.

15. Waters, "Whose Salvation? Which Eschatology?," 170–71.

the human will to achieve perfection, unaided by God's grace.[16] Furthermore, these ideas may give rise to a concerning morality. A Manichean view that shows a hatred for the body and embodiment may easily justify neglect or abuse of the physical. Similarly, the Pelagian quest for perfection may justify an elimination or prevention of anything not considered so, thus fueling eugenic programs in order to sanitize a race or eliminate anything preventing an idealized human race.[17]

Christian theology on the other hand maintains that the physical body is good, and that embodiment is necessary for personhood, with our creaturehood allowing us to give and receive life, both from God and each other, through our physical bodies. Our embodiment is affirmed by the doctrine of the incarnation and it is the resurrection of Jesus Christ that makes Christian eschatology most starkly different to the transhumanist's eschatology. In the resurrection, the soul is not rescued from the body, but rather it is promised a reunification in the world to come, after death. The crucial difference in these worldviews is that while transhumanism seeks a greatly extended longevity or perfection of this life, perhaps culminating in virtual immortality, the Christian consents to a finite and mortal life that will be transcended with an eternal hope after the grave in a truly upgraded body. Therefore, in dishonoring the body, one denies the grace of God that created, sustained, and vindicated the human condition. For a believer, Christ is our exemplar: he was the word made flesh; not flesh made data.[18]

3.2 THE IMPACT OF SIN ON EMBODIED HUMANITY

The Christian tradition, drawing from Genesis 1:27, has maintained that humanity is the apex of God's creation, placed over and

---

16. Waters, "Whose Salvation? Which Eschatology?," 170–71.

17. Waters, "Whose Salvation? Which Eschatology?," 170–71.

18. Waters, "Whose Salvation? Which Eschatology?," 172; John 1:14.

above the animal kingdom. Human nature is understood within the concept of the *imago Dei* (created in the image of God). In the Genesis account, our first progenitors, Adam and Eve, were created good, innocent of sin, but with the potentiality of choosing between loving God or turning away from his commands. Through the crafty temptation of the serpent, they chose to ignore God's prohibitions to eat from the tree of knowledge of good and evil, and as a consequence they were exiled from the paradise in Eden. The result of this fall, or original sin, means our human nature inclines to sin, is weakened in its capacities, and is subject to the domination of death. This concupiscence of the human heart, or "inclination to evil,"[19] is humanity's root problem. Accordingly, human persons are in need of redemption by way of a Savior who can mediate a restoration of one's nature to its original holiness before God. Such a conception of the human person is uniquely different to the progressively good evolution of humanity that the transhumanists espouse. To highlight the salient differences between these two conceptions of the person, I will briefly unpack the doctrine of the *imago Dei* and the fall of humankind.

The concept of *imago Dei* is commonly understood to refer to the original uprightness of human nature and its inherent dignity. During the patristic period, Augustine interpreted this concept in terms of human rational faculty mirroring the wisdom of God, with the essential distinctive of human nature as being able to relate to God. Athanasius taught that Adam and Eve enjoyed a perfect relation with God, the Logos, in Eden, when they related to and partook in the very life of God. For the Cappadocians, this meant Adam and Eve were originally free from all the normal weaknesses of human nature subsequent to the fall, including death. Cyril of Jerusalem emphasized that the fall resulted from Adam and Eve's choice, not from necessity. The consequence of this choice was that the image of God in human nature became defaced and disfigured. Furthermore, because Adam was the representative head

---

19. Concupiscence defined as "inclination to evil" in *Catechism of the Catholic Church*, 377.

of humanity, it followed that all of his descendants shared in that defacement of the image of God.[20]

Although Augustine expressed the fall of humanity in terms of the doctrine of original sin, other Greek patristic writers claimed that sin arises from an abuse of free will. Despite varying views on original sin, patristic scholar J. N. D. Kelly identifies three important points that encapsulate the patristic tradition. Firstly, all humanity is understood to be involved in the disobedience of Adam in some mystical unity of species. We are all wounded by Adam's disobedience. Secondly, the fall of Adam is understood to have affected human moral nature, leading to moral weaknesses such as lust, greed, and a propensity to fall short of God's perfect moral law. Finally, Adam's sin is seen to be transmitted to all his posterity in some manner.[21]

Augustine maintains that we are all born with a human nature that has an inherent bias towards sin or a "sinful disposition," and this view supports the biblical understanding of human nature.[22] He uses three analogies to make his point. Original sin is a *hereditary disease*, which is passed down generationally, weakening humanity, and cannot be cured through human agency. Secondly, sin is a *power* that holds us captive, and our liberation can only come by divine grace. Thirdly, sin is an essential *forensic guilt* from breaking God's perfect moral law that is also passed down generationally.[23] Therefore, humanity's frail, weak, and lost condition is met with God's grace, in Christ Jesus, which is offered to redeem us and to restore to us what was lost or defaced in Eden. God's son, the second Adam, was sent to restore the human being to its intended purpose by its Creator.[24] Indeed, it is a glorious gospel: the new creation in Christ being a sort of *Humanity 2.0* initiated by God himself.

20. McGrath, *Christian Theology*, 369–70; Rom 5:12,19.

21. McGrath, *Christian Theology*, 371.

22. Rom 3:10; 6:23; Gal 3:22; 1 John 5:17; John 16:8.

23. McGrath, *Christian Theology*, 373–74; John 15:5.

24. Eph 4:23, 24; Col 3:10; Rom 8:29; 2 Cor 3:18; Col 1:15.

Most transhumanists, however, denounce religion and ignore the impact of sin in humanity. Many believe religion is for Luddites (opposed to new technology or ways of working), a roadblock or obstruction to a human future that is enhanced, even a posthuman future. One definition given is that "transhumanism is the view that humans should (or should be permitted to) use technology to remake human nature."[25] In the words of Simon Young, "the greatest threat to humanity's continuing evolution is theistic opposition to Superbiology in the name of a belief system based on blind faith in the absence of evidence."[26] Although an apologetic defense against this statement is beyond the scope of this chapter, the resistance some theologians have to the idea of altering human nature and disembodying the human condition is a critique of those putting their faith in technological progress alone. As Deane-Drummond says "we need not totally reject . . . technology, but appreciate its proper limits according to particular goals that express the common good."[27] Therefore, Christian faith is not resistant to change per se, and includes a radical transformation of character as well as creativity in this life.

Transhumanists accuse religion of being an impediment in the advance towards cybernetic immortality, saying that religion seeks to provide a palliative comfort for people facing death so that they can come to accept it. Kurzweil boldly wants to defy death and weaponize nanotechnology to defeat it. He seeks to overcome this "deathist" rationalization and wants to sweep traditional religion out of the road.[28] From a biblical worldview, there is no reasonable opposition to progress towards human betterment through medical technology in human health, or even extending one's life through overcoming diseases. However, the biblical vision of resurrection from the dead is at odds with the transhumanist vision of radical life extension or cybernetic immortality. Therefore, notwithstanding that both worldviews agree that humans seek release

25. Campbell and Walker, "Religion and Transhumanism," 1.

26. Young, *Designer Evolution*, 324.

27. Deane-Drummond, *Christ and Evolution*, 285.

28. Kurzweil, *Singularity Is Near*, 372.

from suffering and death, the immortality promised by Kurzweil and others is limited in scope and falls short of the biblical promise of redemption and a new created order, which also promises resurrection and deals with the sin problem.[29]

3.3. NO ACCOUNT FOR MORAL TRANSFORMATION OR JUDGMENT IN THE TRANSHUMANIST'S WORLDVIEW

Transhumanists often conflate biological evolution and technological progress in championing their agenda. However, even leading evolutionary theorists like Mayr, Ernst, Ayala, and Gould deny that evolutionary change brings automatic progress.[30] Theologians also critique the doctrine of progress, but on different grounds: the sinful condition of human hearts left to themselves. Reinhold Niebuhr's "Christian realism"[31] is helpful in challenging the naiveté of the transhumanist's ideology. Following the tradition of Augustine and Luther, Niebuhr speaks of a Christian realism in relation to the sinful condition of humanity and cautions against an overestimation of what we can achieve ourselves, apart from the grace of God. Niebuhr speaks of the ever-present choice between evil and selfishness, and good and altruism, grounded in our basic human freedoms. The resultant choices can be clearly seen throughout human history through wars, violence, genocide, racism, human trafficking, financial greed, and abuse of power.[32]

Niebuhr critiques the doctrine of evolutionary progress with Christian realism. Although the prophets of the Bible viewed human history as a changing and dynamic reality, journeying from promise to fulfillment, it was not without warning and divine judgment. In biblical prophecy, the certainty of a good outcome is not necessarily guaranteed by progress, but by obedience to God's

29. Peters, "Progress and Provolution," 72–73.
30. Peters, "Progress and Provolution," 78.
31. Niebuhr, *Nature and Destiny of Man*, 2:240.
32. Niebuhr, *Nature and Destiny of Man*, 2:241

loving ways. God will judge each player and nation in history. The problem with a blind belief in progress is that it neglects this ambiguity of human freedom, which may choose creative evil as well as creative good. A transhumanist's view that trusts in ongoing progress as a given *good*, with an inherent built-in *telos*, or guiding principle, always leading to betterment, neglects the endless possibilities of both good and evil with which history is filled.[33] Thus it overlooks the issues of human freedom and moral character, both of which are important characteristics of being human.

The computer virus is a good example of how spiritual pathogens are replicated in technology and bear resemblance to sin and its destructive consequences. A virus that is invented to annihilate computer networks has the express purpose to corrupt. Notwithstanding the benefits and blessings of computers and worldwide internet connection, there are still individuals who seek destruction, and no technological advances or increase in human intelligence can change this ever-present human proclivity. A naïve optimism seeks to ignore this human propensity, and an honest recognition of human behavior is needed. In the words of Niebuhr "sin is natural for man in the sense that it is universal but not in the sense that it is necessary."[34] This realism is a challenge for the transhumanist: human nature can't be changed through the augmentation of intelligence.

Theologians maintain that the vision of human flourishing is one of transcendence and includes the judgment of God on the accomplishments of human history. This is not the same as presuming sociological evolution with spiritual progress. Even a cursory view of history reminds us that sophisticated societies can still invent more horrific ways to destroy their neighbors and exalt themselves. Thus, neither cultural nor biological evolution necessarily leads us on an inexorable road to perfection. It follows that technological advance does not inevitably lead to advance in human goodness or achievement either.[35]

33. Peters, "Progress and Provolution," 79.

34. Niebuhr, *Nature and Destiny of Man*, 1:242.

35. Peters, "Progress and Provolution," 80–81.

In concluding this chapter, it is argued that the transhumanist's viewpoint overestimates the goodness of human nature, neglecting the propensity for humans to use neutral or even good things for evil or selfish purposes, resulting in suffering or chaos. Furthermore, there is also the issue of who is funding the technological advances and the risk of subjugating all their achievements to the values and social ethics of those investors, possibly even to the detriment of the wider society. There is no evidence to think that the current selfish human race can transform themselves into an altruistic one, whether by themselves or through technology. The history of economic injustice, ecological foolishness, and the failure to eliminate poverty, racism, and greed are enough to remind us that increased intelligence will not save us from our "sin."[36]

36. Peters, "Progress and Provolution," 82.

CHAPTER 4

Personhood and Human Embodiment

4.1 WHAT DOES IT MEAN TO BE HUMAN? THE IMPORTANCE OF EMBODIMENT FOR PERSONAL IDENTITY IN CHRISTIAN THEOLOGY

The Christian and transhumanist views of the nature of humanity differ in fundamental ways. The dominant view of Christian orthodoxy affirms the essential goodness of creation and the physical world and promises a future reality which includes a renewal and a re-creation of the physical universe.[1] Although there is a diversity of views of the constituent parts of a human being (body/soul or body/mind, etc.), the view shaped by Judeo-Christian heritage regards the human being as a psychosomatic unity. A human person can be said to be an embodied soul, and the mental-spiritual and bodily aspects of a human being are a unity, with the body sharing fully in one's personal dignity.[2] On the other hand, many liberal secularists or those subscribing to a transhuman ideology view the

1. Simut, "Doctrine of the Resurrection of the Body," 31–45.
2. Mercer, "Resurrection of the Body and Cryonics," 2–3.

body not as an aspect of the personal reality of the human being, but rather as an extrinsic instrument of the mind or self, which is considered the true person. This dualism, setting the body against the person, results in a demeaning of the body as something inferior that is used for purely pragmatic purposes.[3] Typically, a Christian worldview highlights the honoring of the human body and the psychosomatic unity of individual identity, and thus contrasts sharply with the disregard for, or indifference towards, the corporeal nature of humanity that transhumanists often espouse. The question as to whether we regard the body as either indispensable or disposable has crucial implications for the way we see the future flourishing of humanity and the ethics that will guide it.[4]

For centuries Western culture has been shaped by a Christian heritage that regarded nature (including humanity) as God's handiwork, and this undergirded a teleological belief that all living things were structured for a purpose or end goal.[5] Each organ of a living creature is wonderfully adapted to the other parts to form a coordinated, goal-directed purpose for the creature and this integrated structure is the hallmark of design. Engineers will use phrases such as "good engineering design" or "reverse engineering," geneticists will speak about DNA being a "database" of genetic information, and astrophysicists will talk about the physical universe as being "fine-tuned" for our existence on the planet. From the perspective of faith, these all point to careful and intentional design. From a Christian viewpoint, the human person and the human body, as part of nature, are also teleological, and the two form an integrated psycho-physical unity. Therefore, there is no dichotomy between "person" and "physical body" and both "declare the glory of God."[6]

Given that our view of the body corresponds to our view of nature, does one understand nature as essentially good and a gift from God to be grateful for, or does one view the body as a

3. Kraftchick, "Bodies, Selves, and Human Identity," 61.

4. Labrecque, "Glorified Body," 2–3.

5. Ps 19:1; Rom 1:20.

6. Pearcey, *Love Thy Body*, 22–23. See also Gen 2:7; 1 Cor 15:45.

prison, with negative limitations to be controlled and conquered? The two-level dualism of personhood theory is akin to the Platonic idea of the primary self as spirit/mind imprisoned by a body, and is, among other things, an attack on the body. A biblical defense of the body is needed to heal this alienation between body and person.[7]

The moral code espoused in the bible presupposes human embodiment and, therefore, respect for the human person is tied to respect for his or her body. Scripture treats body and soul as a unity, with the body being the means by which we interact with God, other persons, and our world.[8] Our bodies are also the means in which our inner souls are made visible to the world. In the words of Meilaender, "the living body is therefore the locus of personal presence."[9] Welton states that the Bible does not separate the body to a lower level of biochemical machine or reduce it to a material object or biophysical entity. Rather, "the body is intrinsic to the person"[10] and their place in the moral and spiritual universe. On this basis, given the evidence of the resurrection of Jesus Christ, Christians believe the body will ultimately be redeemed. The New Testament does not reject the body but argues for its redemption and transformation, along with moral and spiritual transformation.[11] Therefore, a biblical ethic is based on the concept of *imago Dei*: that we are made in God's image as embodied beings, that there is no ultimate division or alienation between our minds and bodily actions, and despite the corruption of sin, God purposes to restore the psychosomatic unity of a person at the resurrection.

Redemption, from a biblical point of view, is cosmic in its ramifications. Paul writes that the whole creation itself groans

7. "The scientific rationalism spearheaded by Descartes is above all an attack on the body. Its first principle is that the human body, together with all matter, shall be seen as an object of power" (Waldstein, "Introduction" 95). See also Kraftchick, "Bodies, Selves, and Human Identity," 61.

8. Ps 32:3 44:25; 63:1; Prov 4:21–22.

9. Meilaender, *Bioethics*, 6.

10. Welton, "Biblical Bodies," 255.

11. Welton, "Biblical Bodies," 255.

under sufferance and brokenness, but that it will be liberated at the end of time, and this deliverance is connected to the freedom and the glory of the children of God.[12] The gospel message is that the whole physical world will be transformed in the eschaton, and humanity will not be saved out of the material creation but rather saved together with the material creation. This promised new earth is a restoration of the physical world into a glorified state, where believers will live in their renewed bodies in a renewed creation (Jesus' resurrection being the firstfruits); they will not be floating around in the universe as wispy, filmy, spiritual ghosts.[13] The Bible presents a very high view of the physical world.

Scripture does, however, explain why at times we feel estranged from our bodies or feel the disharmony within them, and this relates to the impact of sin on embodied humanity (as covered in ch. 3.2). This alienation within ourselves and ambivalence towards our bodies harkens back to the fall in Eden. The disharmony one often feels was not our original created state, nor is it the state of our redeemed selves. Paul talks about his struggle with the "body of sin" in Romans 6:6: "knowing this, that our old self was crucified with Him, in order that our body of sin might be done away with, so that we would no longer be slaves to sin." The context makes it clear that the problem is not the body, but *sin*, as the body is merely the site where the battle between good and evil takes place. If one offers one's body to sin, it leads to death. However, offering oneself to obedience results in righteousness.[14] Paul expresses this unwanted alien force of sin within as the "sin which dwells in me"; describing his "flesh" or "carnal" nature as at odds with the spirit or "the law of God in the inner man." However, Paul thanks God that "the law of the Spirit of life in Christ Jesus" has set him free from "the law of sin and death" and promises that we too can overcome.[15] Furthermore, the healing narratives in the Gospels stress the importance of the physical in the kingdom realm,

12. Rom 8:21.

13. Pearcey, *Love Thy Body*, 38–39.

14. Rom 6:16.

15. Rom 7:17; 7:25—8:17; 12:1; 1 Cor 6:20.

and Jesus offers us his body and blood as symbols for partaking of his life, undergirding the dignity of the body. Scripture is replete with bodily images and analogies, symbols, and metaphors for our participation in the spiritual world.[16]

The understanding of the human person as a unity that forms a single entity is deeply ingrained in the church's theology of the body, undergirded by the incarnation, and affirmed in salvation history. The Catholic Church teaches that one should neither despise nor dispose of their body, but ought to "regard the body as good and to hold it in honour since God has created it and will raise it up on the last day."[17] Therefore one's identity is rooted in the composite of body and soul as a person, and this continuity of personhood goes on even into the afterlife, where the body and soul will be reunited after death. Accordingly, in Christian theology, the human body is indispensable.[18] John Paul II encapsulates the Catholic position when he states that the value of the human body is connected to "what the human person *is*, rather than what the human person *has*."[19] Tertullian refers to the body as "the hinge of salvation,"[20] and the God who chose to dwell among us in the flesh in order to redeem our bodies can be said to be the distinctive sign of the Christian faith. Therefore, Christian theology depends on the corporeal body for humanhood: both now, in the future, and in the hereafter.

16. Pearcey, *Love Thy Body*, 43–44.
17. *Catechism of the Catholic Church*, n364.
18. Labrecque, "Glorified Body," 5.
19. John Paul II, *Man and Woman*, 681 (emphasis original).
20. *Catechism of the Catholic Church*, n1015.

4.2 WHAT DOES IT MEAN TO BE HUMAN? BIOLOGICAL MACHINE AND TRANSHUMAN IDEOLOGY

Will *homo sapiens* be replaced by some posthuman species (i.e., *homo cyberneticus*[21] or *techno sapiens*[22]) in the future, as transhumanists claim? Since the Enlightenment period, modern science has increasingly viewed humans essentially as rational beings. In recent history, with the rise of neuroscience, advanced technology, computers, and artificial intelligence, it has become common to compare our physical brains to hardware and our minds to software, resulting in a conception of the human person as *a biological machine* or a *biological computer*. In this view, humans are understood to be preprogrammed by biological factors to act in certain ways. This understanding raises questions of human freedom and dignity.

The view of humanity as a machine finds its roots in the eighteenth century in the work of La Mettrie, a French physician and materialist philosopher who wrote the book *Man a Machine*.[23] La Mettrie denied the existence of the soul as separate from matter, and extended Descartes's argument that animals were mere automations, or machines, to human persons. In the Newtonian age, the universe was conceived as being governed by logical and understandable laws, and this was the basis for much Enlightenment thought. This was questioned by the rise of Darwinism in the nineteenth century and the emergence of quantum physics in the twentieth century, both of which saw randomness and chance as drivers of change. However, the belief in a more deterministic model had not completely vanished, especially for neuroscientists. In recent decades the human brain has been compared with digital computers as they both contain circuits for input and output, a central processing unit, and memory.[24] Many physicists, biologists

21. Peters, "Progress and Provolution," 67.
22. Jackson, "Image of God as *Techno Sapiens*," 289–302.
23. La Mettrie, *Man a Machine*.
24. Luo, "Why is the Human Brain so Efficient?"

and philosophers today conceive of the human person as simply a biological computer, with no real ontological distinction between the artifact and the living being.[25]

The recent explosion of knowledge in neuroscience regarding brain function has impacted human self-understanding in profound ways, accompanied by claims of absolute biological determinism. Not only is the brain involved in every aspect of human functioning, but some would go further and say that our emotions, thoughts, and personalities are "nothing but" what goes on in our brains.[26] Much reporting of recent discoveries in neuroscience seems to suggest our genes and physiology are controlling us, and that genes are linked with specific behaviors, emotions, or attitudes that are beyond one's conscious control.[27] Hewlett says that human behavior is completely determined by our genes and all behaviors are merely reflections of some survival advantage in a section of our DNA,[28] while neuroscientist Critchlow argues there is no such thing as free will—it is all an illusion.[29] According to this worldview, we are nothing but a collection of chemicals and electrical impulses that operate in predetermined ways.

There is no agreed theory as to the nature of consciousness in a human being. Two different notions emerge within the reductive physicalist's view (those who hold the view that the mind is reducible to physics and chemistry alone). One view is that brain science can access consciousness and explain it in physical terms, and the other is that consciousness is illusory.[30] Therefore, both these naturalist views believe that consciousness is synonymous with brain activity: it is the brain. However, Dirckx argues, based on clinical studies of near-death and brain-death activity, that consciousness is different to brain activity, although the two work

25. Burdett, "Image of God and Human Uniqueness," 8–9. See also Dirckx, *Am I Just My Brain?*, 55–74.

26. Watts, "Multifaceted Nature of Human Personhood," 57.

27. Alexander, "Genes, Determinism and God," 1.

28. Hewlett, "What Does It Mean to Be Human?"

29. Tucker, "Neuroscientist Dr Hannah Critchlow."

30. See Dennett, "Explaining the Magic of Consciousness," 7–8.

closely together. Thus, a reductive physicalist approach to consciousness is inadequate. She maintains that consciousness itself cannot be reduced to merely physical processes in the brain: they are not identical.[31]

Harrari, an evolutionary materialist, claims "humans are merely biological organisms driven by instinct to seek pleasure."[32] He concludes that there is no Creator endowing us with "human rights" and that the concept of equal rights is a "Christian myth." In his follow-up book, *Homo Deus*, he examines the possible impact of biotechnology and artificial intelligence innovation on *Homo sapiens*, promoting the beginning of a new bionic or semicomputerized form of human. Most transhumanists, like Harrari, adopt this two-level secular ethic that makes a distinction between being human and being a person with rights. However, the question arises: How would this philosophy play out in a future society if all humans were not considered equal? What would be the concept of justice, if any, for those who were poor, vulnerable, and oppressed? Following this reasoning, if humans are nothing special and not made in the *imago Dei*, then it is fine to use technology to alter them, and/or create a new stage of life beyond humanity. After all, why not take charge of evolution through genetic engineering, if humans are *"only currents in the drift of genes?"*[33] Therefore, how we conceive of ourselves as human beings matters: it matters significantly and profoundly in issues of ethics and human flourishing in the future. This will be discussed further in chapter 6.

Transhumanist enthusiasts promote a vision of a bioengineered utopia in which we will be liberated from our human limitations and wealthy parents will be able to afford genetic improvements so extensive that they will create a new race: *posthumans*. Once the human body has been reduced to a mechanism on the level of a gadget, it is an easier step to normalize experimentation with DNA and gene editing. At this point some may note the concern of the return of eugenics and recoil at the tragic

31. Dirckx, *Am I Just My Brain?*, 39–50.

32. Harrari, *Sapiens*, 108–10.

33. Gray, *Straw Dogs*, 6 (emphasis mine).

results of this under Nazi rule. Transhumanists respond by saying the new eugenics will be based on choice. Parents can choose their offspring's genetic traits.[34] Bostrom, the leading transhumanist at Oxford, says "human nature is a work-in-progress, a half-baked beginning that we can learn to remould in desirable ways."[35] But who decides what is desirable? And will changes of such magnitude realistically remain in the hands of parents? If it becomes possible to remold human nature itself, doesn't this bring up red flags of possible tyranny?

Another prominent transhumanist advocate is geneticist Lee Silver,[36] who unfolds a utopian scenario for the future that some might deem a coercive dystopia. He speaks of humanity bifurcating into two separate races. There is, firstly, the ruling caste, who are the controllers of society (genetic *Ubermenschen*: super-persons), and then there is the group who become the low-paid laborers and service providers (*Untermenschen*: sub-persons). This scenario should disturb us. Once we deny that humans have unique dignity simply because they are human and made in the image of God, we have opened the door for tyranny and exploitation in "justifiable" terms. As Adler warns "groups of superior men [will] be able to justify their enslavement, exploitation, or even genocide of inferior human groups, on factual and moral grounds akin to those that we now rely on to justify our treatment of the animals we harness as beasts of burden."[37] These scenarios call to mind the plotline of countless dystopian movies.[38]

At the far end of the spectrum of transhuman ideology are those who hope to transcend the body altogether. As mentioned previously, Kurzweil believes humanity can achieve a form of immortality through downloading the brain into a computer, making a "digital immortality" possible. Kurzweil states "we will gain

---

34. Pearcey, *Love Thy Body*, 97–98.

35. Bostrom, as quoted in Pearcey, *Love Thy Body*, 98.

36. Silver, *Remaking Eden*.

37. Adler, *Difference of Man*, 264.

38. Blockbuster Hollywood films such as *Lucy, Her, Transcendence, Limitless, Ex Machina, Advantageous, Upgrade.*

power over our fates. Our mortality will be in our own hands. We will be able to live as long as we want . . . by the end of this century, the non-biological portion of our intelligence will be trillions of trillions of times more powerful than unaided human intelligence."[39] Furthermore, he says "the whole idea of a 'species' is a biological concept" and "what we are doing is transcending biology."[40] Bostrom states that if we could build a new, superintelligent machine brain that far surpasses the capacity of any human brain, then "as the fate of the gorillas now depends more on us humans than on the gorillas themselves, so the fate of our species would depend on the actions of the machine superintelligence."[41]

Estulin,[42] author of *TransEvolution: The Coming Age of Human Deconstruction*, states we are on the cusp of the greatest evolutionary change in the history of mankind. In an interview he said

> I can tell you without a doubt that the generations of children who are being born right now are the last truly 100 percent human generation of human beings on the planet. Their children will be transhuman children – post-human man-machines, cyborgs, and beings who are not totally human as a result of synthetic biology. It's absolutely inevitable – the whole idea of merging man and machine."[43]

Estulin believes what is coming will revolutionize the very definition of humanity.

Another influential futurist, Martine Rothblatt, also promotes a similar anti-body ideology in her book *Virtually Human*.[44] Rothblatt's book proposes a digital database of your life to be used to create a "mindclope"[45] (a digital consciousness that will survive

39. Kurzweil, *Singularity Is Near*, 9.

40. Kurzweil, Quoted in Pearcey, *Love Thy Body*, 99.

41. Bostrom, *Superintelligence*, vii.

42. Estulin, *TransEvolution*.

43. Estulin interview with Troy Anderson, quoted in McGuire and Anderson, *Babylon Code*, 122.

44. Rothblatt, *Virtually Human*.

45. Quoted in Pearcey, *Love Thy Body*, 99.

the death of your body). If one prefers a flesh-and-blood body, according to Rothbatt, they are guilty of "fleshism."[46] Furthermore, transgenic technologies (creating new lifeforms across species, including human-animal hybrids) are already being used in experiments and open the way for the refashioning of human nature itself. Why not enhance human capabilities and create a posthuman race? We will be able to manufacture and design a human being in the laboratory, taking the DNA of anything and creating organisms that never existed before: new life forms. As a result, the nature of humanity would be up for negotiation.

The value of the human body and its integration in one's personhood is a central point of contention between the Christian and transhumanist ideologies. For the transhumanist, the future leads to a posthuman species that includes the demeaning and disparaging of the flesh-and-blood body. In this view, we are biological machines that can be tampered with, improved upon, and even surpassed. In contrast, Christianity emphasizes a sanctification of the soul, physical embodiment in the world to come, and a continuity of personal identity into the afterlife. Depending on what view one takes (biological machine vis-à-vis *imago Dei*), the ethical implications for the future of humanity are momentous. I will now turn to the pivotal significance of resurrection for Christian understanding, and that will lead, in chapter 6, to a final revisiting of the ethical issues raised so far.

---

46. Quoted in Pearcey, *Love Thy Body*, 99.

CHAPTER 5

The Doctrine of Bodily Resurrection

5.1 *A CHRISTIAN THEOLOGY OF RESURRECTION*

Christian theology affirms, for followers of Christ, an eschatological resurrection of the body that is both glorious and in harmony with the promise of a new heaven and earth where all things will be reconciled back to God. The resurrection stands in stark contrast to the cybernetic immortality proposed by the radical transhumanists: that is, mere disembodied intelligence. Regardless if such intelligence could reside in a robotic or virtual body, such a posthuman entity's body would be *qualitatively different* from the resurrection hope that the Bible holds out for the human being.[1] The major ecumenical creeds contain statements about resurrection and stress its centrality to Christian faith. Belief in Jesus' resurrection enables and requires us to believe that one day we will be raised in an embodied existence for all eternity, thus our bodies cannot be unimportant or inherently bad.[2] Indeed, faith in the resurrection is axiomatic to the Christian faith as Scripture says if we

---

1. Mercer, "Bodies and Persons," 27.
2. Gooder, *Body*, 57.

do not believe Christ is raised, our faith is futile.[3] Although there is ongoing debate about the when and how of bodily reintegration, and whether there is an "intermediate state" where souls await their bodily resurrection at the last judgment, the overall consensus is that bodily resurrection means "that the personal identity established in an embodied history is raised up into a transphysical reality."[4]

However, resurrection must be understood in the context of "the new creation." A central tenet of Christian faith is God's intervention in the world by Christ to inaugurate a new kingdom and a new age. This new age in Paul's language is "the new creation."[5] Gooder, drawing on insights from N. T. Wright, argues there are three vital elements for understanding what Paul spoke about in the resurrection passage of 1 Corinthians 15. These are: (1) the dead would be raised into a new era, the new creation; (2) the general resurrection would take place when the new creation came fully into being; and (3) that Jesus' resurrection began (but did not bring to completion) that new creation.[6]

Paul significantly contrasts between the old creation and the new creation. The old, symbolized by Adam and marked by sin and the need for law, has been superseded by the new, symbolized by Christ, marked by redemption. The former will fade; the latter will last forever. What is significant here is that bodies are spoken of in both the old creation and the new age to come. However, the bodies we now have fit the old creation, and our new bodies will fit the new creation.[7] Even though Paul's writings are full of contrasts this must be distinguished from an irreconcilable body-and-soul dualism. Paul is thoroughly monotheistic: the only opposing force to God is evil. The created order does not stand in opposition to God. Indeed, the created world, or cosmos, is fully dependent on

3. 1 Cor 15:12–17.

4. Prusak, "Bodily Resurrection," 64.

5. 2 Cor 5:17.

6. Gooder, *Body*, 45. See also Wright, *Paul and the Faithfulness of God*, 1043–1268.

7. Gooder, *Body*, 46, 55.

God and is being reconciled to God.[8] Humanity, along with all of creation, awaits the final consummation.[9] As Wright states, "the resurrection, in the full Jewish and early Christian sense, is the ultimate affirmation that creation matters, that embodied human beings matter."[10]

However, the body spoken of in Scripture is more than mere physicality. Although there is a diversity of views of the constituent parts of a human being, the widely regarded Judeo-Christian view is that a human being is a psychosomatic unity. Aquinas's concept of the human being as being the profound and enduring unity of a soul informing the body and actualizing it remains influential as he states, "it is through the soul that the body becomes a being in act" and "the soul is the form of the animated body."[11] Rahner, when asked what is the fundamental meaning of "resurrection of the dead," stated "body (*fleisch*) means the whole man in his proper embodied reality. Resurrection means, therefore, the termination and perfection of the whole man before God, which gives him 'eternal life.'"[12] He rejected the notion that "lack of relation to matter and nearness to God must increase in direct ratio," but rather accepted that in death the soul became pancosmic (relating to the cosmos as a whole) not acosmic (denying the temporal world).[13] Ratzinger also distinguished the biblical doctrine of resurrection, which views the human person as an undivided unity, with the immortality of the soul only, as espoused by the Greeks. He states "we live our corporality with a new intensity and feel it as the indispensable mode of realization of the one being of man. From this angle we can understand afresh the biblical message, which promises immortality not to a separated soul but to the whole man."[14] Ratzinger proposed that the real hope of the gospel was

---

8. 2 Cor 5:19.

9. Rom 8:19–23.

10. Wright, *Resurrection of the Son of God*, 3:737.

11. Aquinas, *Summa Contra Gentiles*, 2, 57, 14–15.

12. Rahner, "Resurrection of the Body," 2:210–11.

13. Rahner, *On the Theology of Death*, 19–20.

14. Ratzinger, *Introduction to Christianity*, 268–69.

"an immortality of the person, of the *one* creation man" that "goes on existing, even if transformed."[15]

The precise way in which our dead bodies are taken up again into resurrection is unclear, however we can see a glimpse of the heavenly otherness of such a body in Jesus' own resurrection body, as recorded in the gospels. O'Collins[16] notes that when the resurrected Christ emerged from the invisible realm to appear before his disciples in his "spiritual body," although his physical presence was real,[17] it was no mere body from the old creation, nor a reanimation of a corpse.[18] Jesus, although able to eat and drink with his disciples, had been freed from the natural limitations of time, space, and matter. He walked through walls and appeared and reappeared at will on the earth.

O'Collins, noting scientific notions of the interchangeability of energy and matter, says Jesus' resurrection liberated him to enter into bodily relationships "with the universe of men and things," enjoying relations with all places and all times.[19] He goes on to state that resurrection will mean "the full personalizing and spiritualizing of matter, not its abolition. Through the Holy Spirit the human spirit will completely dominate matter. The body will clearly express and serve the glorified spirit of human beings."[20] He offers four helpful points to envisage our future bodiliness: *participation, communication, continuity,* and *salvation.* The entrance of our bodies into the physical world makes us participants in the cosmos, and in relation to God. Our bodies allow us to communicate with others and express ourselves. Despite the massive bodily changes during the course of our life, our personal identity continues through and is connected to our bodily identity. We remain the same person and are/have the same body. Finally, our salvation will be experienced in our bodiliness: it will be the focal

---

15. Ratzinger, *Introduction to Christianity*, 270–71 (emphasis original).

16. O'Collins, *What Are They Saying?*, 49–51.

17. Luke 24:39.

18. Luke 24:42–43; 1 Cor 15:39–41.

19. O'Collins, *What Are They Saying?*, 76–78.

20. O'Collins, *Jesus Risen*, 181–82, 225–26.

point where we experience eternal grace or misery.[21] O'Collins states that "resurrection brings matter its most intense participation in the life of God. By being raised from death, human beings as embodied spirits will not only belong again to the universe but also in a new way will share in divine life."[22] Thus, Jesus, in his resurrection, manifested his glorified humanity; that is, his entire embodied history lived on and was transfigured into his risen existence, which the Christian can likewise hope for.

Some widely agreed-upon statements about the resurrection have been documented in the International Theological Commission's document and are a useful summary. They are:

> (i) resurrection is not a return to this life or reanimation; (ii) the resurrection concerns the whole individual and not only the body or the disembodied soul; (iii) the resurrection is not only an event happening to the individual but also an ecclesial and cosmic event; and (iv) there is both radical continuity and radical discontinuity between the present life and the future.[23]

This biblical worldview, which begins in a glorious creation, finds its fulfillment in the vision of a "new heaven and a new earth,"[24] that is, both a continuous and radically transformed heaven and earth. Included in this vision is the resurrected state of a believer who now has a spiritual body (*soma pneumatikon*).[25] Thus, a person's future state is not as an eternal soul detached from a body, but rather as a body that has been transformed, with greater capacities: one that has both continuity with the preresurrection body, but qualitative differences. Jesus was raised with a glorious body and Paul believed what happened to Jesus has become inextricably entwined with what will happen to Jesus' followers.[26]

21. O'Collins, *Jesus Risen*, 182–84.
22. O'Collins, *Jesus Risen*, 184–85.
23. Cited in Prusak, "Bodily Resurrection," 97.
24. Rev 21:1.
25. 1 Cor 15.
26. Mercer, "Bodies and Persons," 27–28.

5.2 RESURRECTION VERSUS TRANSHUMAN IMMORTALITY

Both Radical Life Extension (RLE—embodied immortality) and Cybernetic Immortality (CI—disembodied immortality) would only extend our current existence indefinitely, [27] however upgraded this existence could be. Neither of these aspirations come near to the transformation of the human person in the new creation that is promised by the New Testament. Neither technology is able to deal with the sin problem in the human heart, which is resolved by death and resurrection, not RLE or CI. As history reveals, there has been a propensity to use scientific discoveries for evil as well as good, either on oneself or others, so the ethical uses of such technology must be taken seriously. It is feasible, if not probable, that these technologies could fall into the wrong hands at some stage and be wielded over humanity in oppressive ways with disastrous consequences. The idea of radical enhancement of the human person, or perfectibility, that is often espoused by transhumanism is vastly different to the new creation promised to us by Christ. The transformation of the Christian is undertaken supernaturally by the power of God, whereas the superhuman of the transhumanists is created through technology and/or a superintelligence, devoid of spiritual life.

The posthuman archetype typically promotes images of hyperfunctionality and superhumanity. This emphasis on power is in stark contrast to the glorified body of Jesus, which demonstrates a "recovery-of-the-body" motif for what follows death.[28] Although transfigured and granted incorruptibility, the body with which Jesus returned was a body that others recognized as him: it was truly physical and bore the marks of his crucifixion. Jesus says "look at my hands and feet" and "see that it is I myself . . . touch me and see; for a ghost does not have flesh and bones as you see that I have."[29] The wounds on Jesus' body are identifying markers of the sacrifice

27. Meilaender, *Should We Live Forever?*, 53.

28. Labrecque, "Glorified Body," 5.

29. Luke 24:39.

he made and the unique status he has in the cosmos. The aim of the transhumanist is to create a superhuman using genetic or machine enhancement, whereas the goal of the Christian is to come into a fuller realization of the image of God. Therefore, human frailties, dependence, suffering, and vulnerabilities are realities that are meant to lead one to surrender to God and be remade in his image, with a character that has been made pure. This process of sanctification during this life, which may involve suffering, is then completed in glorification after death. Aquinas describes the glorified body as one which is "raised up to the characteristics of heavenly bodies; it will be lightsome, incapable of suffering, without difficulty and labor in movement, and most perfectly perfected by its form."[30] This encapsulates the embodied resurrection hope.

Christian theology speaks of a new state of being in eternity, one that doesn't include the disincarnation of the human person, but rather "the spiritualization of their somatic nature."[31] John Paul II describes perfection as the height of communion in the eschaton, that is, the union of soul and body, as well as communion with God, other persons, and the world the come.[32] For a believer, the hope of resurrection in the new kingdom becomes the anchor for our souls when we are experiencing suffering and death. Resurrection will reverse the misfortunes and injustices suffered by us in our mortal bodies, and this hope can change the way we look at aging, suffering, and death. While there is nothing inherently wrong with using the latest scientific research and technology to alleviate suffering or prolong life, at what point is the dignity of a human being compromised or overrun by a dogmatic imperative for continued existence? What RLE or CI offer us is only life extension in an imperfect or incomplete state. There is no inward transformation of character, no fulfillment of purpose, and no God necessary. In contrast to this, the biblical hope maintains that only God can provide true contentment, fulfillment, and perfection in nature.[33]

30. Aquinas, *Summa Contra Gentiles*, IV.86.6.
31. John Paul II, *Man and Woman*, 66:3 (p. 388), 66:5 (389).
32. John Paul II, *Man and Woman*, 67:2 (391–92), 68:1 (394).
33. Peters, "Radical Life Extension."

Our restless hearts do truly long for immortality, for significance and perfection, but that is because they long for God himself. In Augustine's words, *"you have made us for yourself, and our heart is restless until it rests in you."*[34]

---

34. Augustine, *Confessions*, 3 (emphasis original).

CHAPTER 6

Towards a Christian Ethical Framework for Biotechnological Possibilities

6.1 ETHICS, FLOURISHING, AND THE FUTURE

There is much optimism in transhumanism and a tenacious belief that technology will always deliver the progress we seek. Yet Bostrom, a leading theorist of transhumanism in Oxford, began to see the "existential risks" that an artificial "superintelligence" might pose, which could possibly lead the human race to extinction. He considers various pathways to reach superintelligence: (a) continued development of artificial intelligence, (b) whole-brain emulation (explained in his study with Sandberg), (c) cognitive enhancement of our biology, (d) brain-computer interfaces (presently being developed by Elon Musk's Neuralink), or (e) the strengthening of organizations and networks that increase self-awareness.[1] Bostrom favors the first option as the safest, and the first two as more credible than the others. He reasons that a development of AI would ensure control and enable human values to be programmed into the future superintelligence, so that the

1. Bostrom, *Superintelligence*, 50.

"brute force" of calculations would not gain control or take on ethics in opposition to our own.[2] Bostrom also states it is possible for emulations to replace human beings, but the crucial question this raises is: Do these emulations really exist the same way in which we live as living beings? Furthermore, is it even possible to develop human traits such as empathy and ethics in neural networks and artificial systems?

The creation of social robots to replace human caregivers can only cover the role of another person partially, and can never fully substitute for a human person. One such robot is Paro, who is used in the care of children and the elderly. Paro shows pet-like behavior in that he is pleased when you pat him and whimpers if you treat him badly. He responds if you call him, but unlike a pet he doesn't need to eat and doesn't get dirty, sick, run away, or need much upkeep. Importantly though, Paro cannot exceed his programming; he cannot do anything surprising or unpredictable. The robot lacks an autonomous will and, as such, does not even resemble a living pet. When a cat behaves how it wants instead of how its master instructs, it shows it is a living being endowed with its own will. The only way we could completely substitute the human being is to develop something with intentionality. Alan Turing suggested that the test for verifying an authentic artificial intelligence was its capacity to deceive another, possess intentions autonomous from the creator-designer, and effectively imitate the behavior of a human intelligence. However, the existential risks of such creations are evident.[3]

Bostrom seeks to solve this problem of how to create AIs with intentionality, but without the potential of them misleading their creator-programmers with a plan to destroy the human species, by suggesting we should upload the shared values of our humanity into the emulations. However, this is problematic, as shared values alter over time and differ between worldviews. For example, what if, in becoming free from its programming, it embraced "anti-speciesism as a shared ethical value," and destroyed

2. Paura, "Rapture of the Nerds?," 360.

3. Paura, "Rapture of the Nerds?," 360–62.

us? Furthermore, humans are naturally hostile to being replaced by complete substitutes, so the feasibility of creating an emulation with autonomy and intentionality is unlikely.[4]

The transhumanism vision entails faith in a future universe where immortality is achieved by uploading the pattern of each individual on a digital construct. This achievement is predicated on the assumption that it is feasible for a continuation of one's existence to be brought about through a perfect human brain emulation of that person. If this were to be achieved, humanity would have abdicated the dominion over creation to this new species, in order to extend intelligence throughout the whole universe. However, as yet, the only emulations we have created are imitations such as social robots who, while imitating human emotions, are far from genuine emulations and in contrast to human beings are inferior substitutes created for subservice rather than human equality. If we were able to create intentional and autonomous emulations that were also self-conscious, they would not likely remain as the original, and they could very well develop into a new species not wanting to hybridize with ours.

The transhumanist vision is doomed to fail in perfectly emulating the human species in its most authentic definition because its ideals can only be achieved by escaping into the virtual world of cyberspace. The emulations created would only be pale imitations of us, artificial substitutes never really alive but linked to their creators for functioning, much like a puppet. The future of cybernetic immortality is a nonhuman future. What would remain is merely an intelligence, artificial in nature, and programmed to repeat endlessly what was set by its programmers, who vanished, merely imitating the thoughts and behaviors of irreplaceable humans who have become extinct.[5]

The techno-scientific vision for human civilization is distinctly different from the goal of the Christian life: that is, to imitate Christ. Using the exponential advancements in technology to enhance our bodies and minds to better compete with AI or

4. Paura, "Rapture of the Nerds?," 363.
5. Paura, "Rapture of the Nerds?," 364–65.

eventually be subsumed by it threatens to reduce persons to algorithms or completely annihilate our authentic humanity, especially our compassionate and ethical nature. Such a vision reduces transcendence to physical laws and, at best, promises an earthly utopia for cybernetic beings, bereft of any transcendence. While both the Christian and transhuman worldview may agree that the mortal and finite human condition is not ideal, that human potential has not yet been realized and release from our current condition is sought; and death is a final enemy, the solutions proposed for these problems are vastly different, drawing upon very divergent core beliefs and convictions.[6] Ultimately, they hold out mutually exclusive visions of human flourishing for the future.

6.2 HONORING THE BOUNDARIES OF HUMAN NATURE: CONCERNS REGARDING TRANSHUMANISM

Peters asks, "Can a leopard change its spots? Can the human race remake its own nature so that it leaves sin and death behind?"[7] Ethically speaking, we should not only ask whether humans can eradicate sin in their own nature by means of technology, but conversely, are there human qualities we want to preserve and defend against machine technology, such as human empathy, which can never be fully present in technology? Herzfeld[8] argues that if machine intelligence took over from human intelligence this could result in great loss for humankind. She states that a computer cannot be genuinely empathetic or truly feel emotion due to its lack of a body. Furthermore, according to Christian eschatology, resurrection also belongs to human nature and is its final hope. Peters[9] recommends caution with regards to transhumanistic goals, noting that residual concupiscence inevitably finds ways to manipulate

---

6. Waters, "Whose Salvation? Which Eschatology?," 164.

7. Peters, "Boundaries of Human Nature," 3.

8. Herzfeld, "Empathetic Computers," 34.

9. Peters, "Boundaries of Human Nature," 6–7.

technological advances to the detriment of humanity, as well as to the goal of enhancing humanity. Therefore, strong ethical markers and regulations are called for regarding technology that seeks to alter the boundaries of human nature in fundamental ways.

Childs, drawing upon the work of Ramsey,[10] reflects on the theological and ethical assessments of a posthuman future, and states that Christians should be led by "love's commitment to the common good." In seeking the common good, Childs asks two questions: "(1) how does the commitment to justice take concrete shape in public policies governing the advances in science and technology, and (2) how does the commitment to life and healing speak to the ethical distinction between the uses of biomedical technology for therapy versus for enhancement?"[11] Niebuhr[12] maintains that in the political struggle for societal justice, some elements in the collective human behavior can never be made subject to conscience or reason, and neither can the collective attain what individuals may by holy living. Niebuhr reminds us that the capacity for transcendence inherent in the *imago Dei* requires a God, and that the fulfillment of our destiny and meaningfulness cannot be attained without him. Any attempts to self-divinize lead to idolatry, and identifying meaning with only rationality equates to the deification of reason. Similarly, Tillich[13] explains how the demonic arises when humans distort their own exaltation and raise the finite creature to the status of the infinite. He proffers many examples, including the unconditional demands made by states to control others, and individuals who seek idolization from others. Thus, one could argue that transhumanism endows technology with this sort of salvific meaning or status. Furthermore, MacIntyre contends that morality has largely been lost to emotivism and posits three necessary things for morality: "(1) an understanding of "untutored human nature"; (2) a vision of "man-as-he-could-be-if-he realized-his-telos"; and (3) "the moral

10. Ramsey, *Fabricated Man*, 125.
11. Childs, "Beyond the Boundaries," 8.
12. Niebuhr, *Moral Man and Immoral Society*, xii.
13. Tillich, *Systematic Theology*, 3:103.

precepts required for humanity to reach its telos."[14] Without this Christian realism, the courage to impose strong, ethical parameters would be difficult.

From a theological standpoint, there are many biblical warnings to avert attempts to be like God, apart from his grace and ways. In Eden, the original humans were expelled for their transgression and forbidden to eat of "the tree of life" in their fallen state, lest they become immortal in their sin-inclined status.[15] Subsequently, humanity's hope of immortality could not be realized until a Savior was born into history in the fullness of time, making atonement for the original transgression. However, humans still persisted in seeking independence from the ways of their Creator. A classic biblical example is the construction of the Tower of Babel as a monolithic superstructure reaching to the heavens; a ziggurat designed to make a name for themselves. They sought glory for themselves instead of in relation to God.[16] This act of defiance attracted the ire of God, who confused their languages and dispersed them over the face of the earth. It is easy to see the similarities of vision between this historical event and today's scientists who seek to build an artificial, superintelligent singleton, which acts as a monolithic agency of decision-making for the world. Both of these systems are a quest for the supremacy of humankind to make of themselves what they want; people wanting to trust the creations of their own hands over and above trusting their Creator. However, in contrast, believers are exhorted to imitate Christ, who considered equality with God not something to be grasped at, but submitted to the Father in all things, including death.[17] Christ is our example of perfect humanity. These biblical prohibitions not to seek out self-divinization seem clear.

On the other side of the argument are the transhumanists. The transhumanist website *Humanity+* states its goals are compatible with the general ethic of promoting health and well-being

14. MacIntyre, *After Virtue*, 52.

15. Gen 3:22–24.

16. Gen 11:1–9.

17. Phil 2:5–11.

and saving lives. Therefore they maintain that cryonics (freezing corpses with the hope of a possible resurrection in the future) and healthspan-extension are a priority. They state they want individuals to be free to make their own choices concerning the use of technology and science. They hold out a world where non-enhanced and enhanced people can peaceably live together, or perhaps the provision of a separate community where those who wish to remain human without enhancements could live.[18] However, important questions remain concerning this vision: Will these technologies have a price tag that only a few can afford? How can we know enough information about the consequences of some of these technologies for us to make proper decisions? Will not this sort of subjective choice and unrestrained autonomy lead to chaos, or no morality at all? How will justice be upheld? McKenny agrees with MacIntyre that the loss of a telos for human fulfill-ment threatens ethical considerations and states "no account can be given of the good that has no relation to our human nature, and so the transhumanist conception of the good must necessarily be an empty one."[19] This is reflected in the *Humanity+* website, which boldly states, "some posthumans may find it advantageous to jettison their bodies altogether and live as information patterns on vast super-fast computer networks."[20] Thweatt-Bates draws a parallel between the "disembodied transhumanist anthropology" and "neoplatonic Christian theological views of the body as evil, seductive matter,"[21] and critiques transhumanists' ideals as a valo-rizing of Enlightenment humanism. [22] An anthropology where the physical body is seen as inherently flawed does not add to a vision of future flourishing.

The essential characteristic of humans being made in the image of God is that our personhood is derivative from, and

18. See *Humanity+* website: www.humanityplus.org.

19. McKenny, "Transcendence, Technological Enhancement, and Chris-tian Theology," 187.

20. Humanity+, "Transhumanist FAQ," para. 16.

21. Thweatt-Bates, "Artificial Wombs and Cyborg Births," 109.

22. Thweatt-Bates, "Artificial Wombs and Cyborg Births," 102.

dependent on, our Creator and defined by its relation to God. As Tillich reminds us, true faith concerns us with what is truly ultimate, while idolatrous faith elevates the finite to the status of ultimacy, with the inescapable consequence being that of "existential disappointment."[23] To seek the infinite in human finitude or the ultimate in the conditional, is a profound error that leads to ultimate estrangement. Therefore, the estrangement of body from spirit is merely a subset of the existential lostness of humans from the divine connection. It is indeed a profound loss.

6.3 ASPECTS OF HUMAN NATURE WE OUGHT TO PRESERVE AND DEFEND

Can artificial intelligence and cybernetic immortality created by humans ever be superior to the human intelligence and the telos of the human person that God created? The two worldviews of the transhumanist and the Orthodox Christian have very different underlying presumptions. Stephen Hawking believed that at some point we would arrive at ASI (Artificial Super Intelligence) and AI would take off on its own at such an exponential rate that it would redesign itself, while humans would be superseded due to their slow biological evolution. If this scenario played out, only cybernetic immortality would remain for anyone who was once human. However, this rationale presumes that a human is no different from a computer and merely a brain. Hawking's position, common with many in the transhumanist movement, presumes "(i) evolution (2) non-existence of God, and (3) humanity as no different to objects."[24]

Christians derive their ethical stance and core convictions about reality, including the human person, from a biblical perspective. It is proposed that four broad biblical pillars can guide us into preserving and upholding the dignity and integrity of the

---

23. Tillich, *Systematic Theology*, 3:103.
24. Ng, "How Artificial Super-Intelligence Is Today's Tower of Babel."

human person, while advancing and improving our quality of life on earth, in light of current and proposed technologies:

1. Uphold the *imago Dei* in all human beings, validating people as bearers of God's image and the head of the created order on earth.[25] Technological advances should be used in order to help and bless humanity, not destroy or divide it, nor transgress boundaries of species in the created order.

2. Uphold the biblical mandate for humans to subdue the earth and all creatures within it,[26] including dominion over any man-made artificial intelligence and all technological creations of humans. This assertion ensures the AI agenda is subject to humankind and challenges an agenda that seeks to supersede the human species.[27]

3. Uphold the integrity of the human person as a psychosomatic unity.[28] In upholding the hope of resurrection from the dead in a unity of person, the body should not be disposed of, or separated from the soul by human intervention. While AI seeks to digitize a portion of human intelligence, human consciousness (or the human spirit), which connects one to God, cannot ever be replicated by AI.

4. Uphold moral accountability of persons, maintaining appropriate laws and penalties necessary for an ethical and just society. Civil liberties should not be made redundant by technology or humans made plastic through genetic engineering.

If the ultimate ethic is love for one another, technological advancements and AI should only be used as tools of service for the benefit of humankind. Without this Judeo-Christian ethic, and a recognition of the problems raised in the development of AI, unfettered technological expansion has the potential to be used to serve nefarious agendas that may only benefit an elite class. Therefore,

25. Gen 1:27.
26. Gen 1:28.
27. Ng, "How Artificial Super-Intelligence Is Today's Tower of Babel."
28. 1 Thess 5:23.

clear "technomoral virtues,"[29] laws, and policies are needed for the future flourishing of all.

29. Vallor, *Technology and the Virtues*, 5.

CHAPTER 7

Concluding Thoughts

THIS BOOK HAS DEMONSTRATED that there are some core convergences between the transhumanist ideology and Christian orthodoxy. These include the desire to live in a perfect world where there is no death and suffering, and a yearning to attain immortality. Living forever has always been an ideal that humans have dreamed of and longed for; perhaps an echo of the divine image that we were created with.

There are also fundamental differences. Christians want to be better human persons; transhumanists want to be trans- or posthumans. What it means to be fully human is very different to each group. There are profound and systemic differences in these two worldviews, including radical human enhancement goals that are incompatible with the final eschatological promise that is offered to us by Christ in the resurrection and the world to come.[1] Transhumanists want to move beyond being human as we know it, including shedding the biological body. Both worldviews have deification claims but they are based on mutually exclusive goals, because at the foundation of their visions lay diverse and competing anthropologies. A Christian's theological or ethical contribution to the discussions of the use of future technology will necessarily caution against unbridled use of technological possibilities on the

---

1. 1 Cor 15:54–55.

human body and person, particularly if it seeks to change the nature of the human identity given to them by God. Transhumanists hold out cybernetic immortality as the ultimate vision; Christians hold out resurrection from the dead in a corporeal body as the ultimate vision.

The Transhuman ideology is not necessarily a new idea. Julian Huxley believed the nature of life was to overcome itself and was the first to coin the phrase "transhumanism" in his 1957 essay "Transhumanism." Huxley integrated Gregor Mendel's theory of genetics with Darwin's theory of evolution in his book *Evolution: The Modern Synthesis*,[2] first published in 1942. What resulted was Neo-Darwinism: a notion that humans are only a phase in the evolutionary chain and not the end point. Therefore, it was imperative that we fight entropy, seek to improve ourselves, and transcend our own species. Following on from Nietzsche's "will to power"[3] and Schopenhauer's "will to live,"[4] and a culture that portends the death of God, transhumanism has become the new successor to the Christian promise of the afterlife, at least for the secular populace. Leading transhumanists, such as Kurzweil and Bostrom, now see this ideology as a technological imperative.

In contrast to the above ideology, the biblical vision of the resurrection demonstrates that human deification can only be achieved through the divine initiation of grace that no amount of human effort or technology could parallel.[5] Whereas transhumanism seeks to reduce the importance or prominence of the physical body, ignoring or denying the glory of embodiment, Christianity holds out a hopeful future where God's full realized kingdom will usher in the swallowing up of all suffering, sickness, and death in the coming eschaton. Here the human body is granted incorruptibility when God affects a reunion of soul and body, albeit transformed and renewed. Therefore, Christianity upholds that

2. Huxley, *Evolution*.

3. Nietzsche, *Will to Power*.

4. Schopenhauer, *Will to Live*.

5. McKenny, "Transcendence, Technological Enhancement, and Christian Theology," 185.

the only way to overcome death and sin is by God's grace, which necessitates submitting to death as a doorway to a new creation and an incorruptible life.

In each chapter of this book, I have argued that:

1. Transhumanist ideas and their influence are ubiquitous in popular culture, and we are heading towards greater and greater integration with technology and a disembodied human experience.

2. The eschatology of the transhumanist, positing a posthuman entity dislodged from its biological body in the future, is vastly different from the biblical eschatology of immortality of the entire human person as espoused by Christ. I, therefore, conclude that these different visions yield mutually exclusive goals for human flourishing.

3. Our creaturehood means our lives are contingent on a Creator and this is a good and positive truth that gives us divine purpose and a greater understanding of the temporary suffering and death we need to endure in this world. Some limitations and suffering engender virtues in our persons, such as compassion, love for the other, and the realization of the interdependence of all things—all of which are good outcomes. Therefore, we should not seek to overcome those intrinsic limitations that relate to our human person, nor replace every limitation with unfettered freedom through technology.[6]

4. The root problem of most of the suffering of humanity can be traced to the propensity in the heart of a person to sin, or to be selfish and greedy, thus neglecting to love one's neighbor.[7] The problem, therefore, is not merely a lack of intelligence or physical perfection that can be overcome or conquered

6. Deane-Drumond, "Taking Leave of the Animal?" 115. Thweatt-Bates, "Cyborg Selves," 152. Burdett, "Eschatology and the Technological Future," 238.

7. McGrath, *Christian Theology*, 369–71; Niebuhr, *Nature and Destiny of Man*, 2:241.

by technology alone, so one need not fear death per se (as it presents a gateway to a higher life), but rather an immortal life without the eradication of sin is more to be feared.

5. The biblical hope and promise of resurrection of the dead as purified and glorified human beings, who retain the unity of body-soul-spirit, is the ultimate and superior hope for future humanity.[8] This goal includes the will/choice being preserved and perfected through the sanctifying and glorifying process of transformation through God's prevenient grace.

6. In the assessment and implementation of various technological advancements to benefit human beings in the future, it is recommended that possibilities be filtered through a grid that endeavors to uphold our human dignity by preserving (1) the *imago Dei* in all persons, (2) humanity's dominion over any artificial intelligence, (3) unity of body and soul, and (4) accountability to God and others as paramount in humanity's bid to improve life and community for future human flourishing and progress.

As humans, we long and yearn for eternal life and immortality. Our deepest desires and fears are wrapped up in the paradox at the heart of the gospel: that is, it is only by losing our lives that we gain them.[9] Biblical theology posits that there is only one way to reverse the cosmic upheaval we are currently experiencing. It is through union with the Messiah, Christ Jesus, whose atoning death has already rippled throughout the cosmos, beginning a healing of the entire creation. Scripture declares there will be a day when the Lord will fully reconcile all things, whether on earth or in heaven, as he alone holds the entire creation together.[10]

I have argued that this final and real eschatological promise offered to us by God far outweighs any artificial or technological copy of human beings that mankind can create. Therefore, this calls for active resistance to the hollow promises of cybernetic

8. Labrecque, "Glorified Body," 166; Gooder, *Body*, 57.

9. John 12:25; Mark 8:35; Luke 14:26.

10. Col 1:16–19.

immortality, and for a vigorous defense of the hope-filled resurrection promises of the gospel. In this hour, when exponential technological possibilities abound, and immortality is eagerly sought apart from God, what is needed most is a bold proclamation of, and faith in, the scriptural promises of a resurrected life of eternal value: a life we all long for, both now and in the future.

Bibliography

Adler, Mortimer J. *The Difference of Man and the Difference It Makes*. New York: Fordham University Press, 1967.

Alexander, Denis. "Genes, Determinism and God." *Cambridge Papers* 22.4 (2013) 1–4.

Aperture. "Neuralink: Merging Man and Machine." *YouTube*, January 10, 2020. 12:51. https://www.youtube.com/watch?v=ojOjh6l wp9w&feature=share&fbclid=IwAR006KBfoiQGrOBEDjeG-ME3Bxp7YWQeoNFBTRA4HPgR-tzST5AzpFk9m9A.

Aquinas, Thomas. *Summa Contra Gentiles*. Translated by Charles J. O'Neil. New York: Hanover House, 1955–57. https://isidore.co/aquinas/ContraGentiles.htm.

———. *Summa Theologiae*. https://www.ccel.org/a/aquinas/summa/home.html.

Augustine. *Confessions*. Translated by Henry Chadwick. Oxford: Oxford University Press, 1991.

Bostrom, Nick. *Superintelligence: Paths, Dangers, Strategies*. Oxford: Oxford University Press, 2014.

———. "Transhumanist Values." *Review of Contemporary Philosophy* 4 (May 2005) 3–14. https://eclass.uoa.gr/modules/document/file.php/PPP566/Bostrom%20-%20Transhumanist%20Values.pdf.

Bugajska, Anna. "Will Postmortal Catholics Have 'The Right to Die'? The Transhumanist and Catholic Perspectives on Death and Immortality." *Forum Philosophicum* 24.2 (2019) 397–433. DOI:10.35765/forphil.2019.2402.17.

Burdett, Michael. *Eschatology and the Technological Future*. London: Routledge, 2015.

———. "The Image of God and Human Uniqueness: Challenges from the Biological and Information Sciences." *The Expositor Times* 127.1 (2015) 3–10.

Burdett, Michael, and Victoria Lorrimar. "Deification and Creaturehood in an Age of Enhancement." *Theology and Science* 16.3 (2018) 247–50. DOI: 10.1080/14746700.2018.1488467.

Campbell, Heidi, and Mark Walker. "Religion and Transhumanism: Introducing a Conversation." *Journal of Evolution and Technology* 14.2 (2005) i–xiv.

Capek, Karel. *R.U.R.* Translated by Paul Selver and Nigel Playfair. Mineola, NY: Dover, 2001.

Catholic Church. *Catechism of the Catholic Church* (1997). https://www.vatican.va/archive/ENG0015/_INDEX.HTM.

Childs, James M., Jr. "Beyond the Boundaries of Current Human Nature: Some Theological and Ethical Reflections on Transhumanism." *Dialog* 54.1 (2015) 8–19.

Cole-Turner, Ronald, ed. *Transhumanism and Transcendence: Christian Hope in an Age of Technological Enhancement.* Washington, DC: Georgetown University Press, 2011.

Deane-Drummond, Celia. *Christ and Evolution.* Minneapolis: Fortress, 2009.

———. "Remaking Human Nature: Transhumanism, Theology, and Creatureliness in Bioethical Controversies." In *Religion and Transhumanism: The Unknown Future of Human Enhancement*, edited by Calvin Mercer and Tracy Trothen, 245–54. Santa Barbara, CA: Praeger, 2015.

———. "Taking Leave of the Animal? The Theological and Ethical Implications of Transhuman Projects." In *Transhumanism and Transcendence: Christian Hope in an Age of Technological Enhancement*, edited by Ronald Cole-Turner, 115–30. Washington, DC: Georgetown University Press, 2011.

De Grey, Aubrey. "The War on Aging." In *The Scientific: Conquest of Death*, edited by Immortality Institute, 29–45. Buenos Aires: Libros EnRed, 2004.

Dennett, Daniel. "Explaining the Magic of Consciousness." *Journal of Cultural and Evolutionary Psychology* 1.1 (2003) 7–8.

Dirckx, Sharon. *Am I Just My Brain?* Oxford: Good Book, 2019.

Drevitch, Gary. "Tinkering with Morality." *Psychology Today*, March 9, 2015. https://www.psychologytoday.com/intl/articles/201503/tinkering-mortality.

Dumouchel, Paul. "Intelligence, Artificial and Otherwise." *Forum Philosophicum* 24.2 (2019) 241–58. DOI:10.35765/forphil.2019.2402.11.

Estulin, Daniel. *TransEvolution: The Coming Age of Human Deconstruction.* Walterville, OR: Trine Day, 2014.

Gay, Craig M. *Modern Technology and the Human Future.* Downers Grove, IL: IVP Academic, 2018.

Gooder, Paula. *Body: Biblical Spirituality for the Whole Person.* London: SPCK, 2016.

Gray, John. *Straw Dogs.* London: Granta, 2002.

Hanson, Robin. *The Age of Em: Work, Love, and Life When Robots Rule the Earth.* Oxford: Oxford University Press, 2016.

Harrari, Yuval Noah. *Homo Deus: A Brief History of Tomorrow.* London: Penguin Random House, 2016.

———. *Sapiens: A Brief History of Humankind.* New York: Harper Collins, 2015.

Hefner, Philip. "The Evolution of the Created Co-Creator." *Currents in Theology and Mission* 15.6 (1988) 512–25.

Herzfeld, Noreen L. "Empathetic Computers: The Problem of Confusing Persons and Things." *Dialog* 54.1 (2015) 34–39.

Hewlett, Martinez. "What Does It Mean to Be Human? Genetics and Human Identity." In *Human Identity at the Intersection of Science, Technology and Religion*, edited by Nancey Murphy and Christopher C. Knight, 147–64. London: Routledge, 2010.

Hollinger, Dennis. "Biotechnologies and Human Nature: What We Should Not Change in Who We Are." *Ethics and Medicine* 29.3 (2013) 173–90.

Humanity+. "Transhumanist FAQ: What Is a Posthuman?" https://www.humanityplus.org/transhumanist-faq.

Huxley, Aldous. *Brave New World*. New York: Harper Perennial, 2006.

Huxley, Julian. *Evolution: The Modern Synthesis*. The Definitive Edition. Cambridge, MA: MIT Press, 2010.

International Theological Commission. "Communion and Stewardship: Human Persons Created in the Image of God." (2004) https://www.vatican.va/roman_curia/congregations/cfaith/cti_documents/rc_con_cfaith_doc_20040723_communion-stewardship_en.html.

Jackson, Antje. "The Image of God as *Techno Sapiens*." *Zygon* 37.2 (2002) 289–302.

John, Mark. "Pandemic Boosts Super-Rich Share of Global Wealth." *Reuters*, December 6, 2021. https://www.reuters.com/business/pandemic-boosts-super-rich-share-global-wealth-2021-12-07/.

John Paul II, Pope. *Man and Woman He Created Them: A Theology of the Body*. Translated by Michael Waldstein. Boston: Pauline, 2006.

Kraftchick, Steven John. "Bodies, Selves, and Human Identity: A Conversation between Transhumanism and the Apostle Paul." *Theology Today* 72.1 (2015) 47–69. DOI: 10.1177/0040573614563530.

Kurzweil, Ray. *The Age of Spiritual Machines: When Computers Exceed Human Intelligence*. New York: Penguin, 2000.

———. *The Singularity Is Near: When Humans Transcend Biology*. New York: Penguin, 2005.

Labrecque, Cory Andrew. "The Glorified Body: Corporealities in the Catholic Tradition." *Religions* 8.9 (2017) 166. DOI: 10.3390/rel8090166.

La Mettrie, Julien Offray de. *Man a Machine* (1748). English translation of *L'homme machine*. http://bactra.org/LaMettrie/Machine/.

Lewis, C. S. *The Abolition of Man*. Glasgow: Collins, 1986.

———. *That Hideous Strength*. London: Harper Collins, 2003.

Luo, Liqun. "Why Is the Human Brain so Efficient? How Massive Parallelism Lifts the Brain's Performance above That of AI." *Nautilus* (April 3, 2018). http://nautil.us/issue/59/connections/why-is-the-human-brain-so-efficient.

MacIntyre, Alasdair. *After Virtue: A Study in Moral Theory*. Notre Dame: University of Notre Dame Press, 1981.

Malapi-Nelson, Alcibiades. "Transhumanism, Posthumanism, and the Catholic Church." *Forum Philosophicum* 24.2 (2019) 369–96. DOI:10.35765/forphil.2019.2402.16.

Mann, Mark H. "The Church Fathers and Two Books Theology." *Biologos* (November 4, 2012). https://biologos.org/articles/the-church-fathers-and-two-books-theology.

McAleer, Graham, and Christopher M. Wojtulewicz. "Why Technoscience Cannot Reproduce Human Desire According to Lacanian Thomism." *Forum Philosophicum* 24.2 (2019) 279–300. DOI:10.35765/forphil.2019.2402.13.

McGrath, Alister E. *Christian Theology*. Oxford: Blackwell, 1995.

McGuire, Paul, and Troy Anderson. *The Babylon Code*. New York: FaithWords, 2015.

McKenny, Gerald. "Transcendence, Technological Enhancement, and Christian Theology." In *Transhumanism and Transcendence: Christian Hope in an Age of Technological Enhancement*, edited by Ronald Cole-Turner, 177–92. Washington, DC: Georgetown University Press, 2011.

Meilaender, Gilbert. *Bioethics: A Primer for Christians*. 3rd ed. Grand Rapids: Eerdmans, 2013.

———. *Should We Live Forever? The Ethical Ambiguities of Aging*. Grand Rapids: Eerdmans, 2013.

Mercer, Calvin R. "Bodies and Persons: Theological Reflections on Transhumanism." *Dialog* 54.1 (2015) 27–33.

———. "The Resurrection of the Body and Cryonics." *Religions* 8.96 (2017) 1–9. DOI:10.3390/rel8050096.

Moravec, Hans. *Mind Children: The Future of Robot and Human Intelligence*. Cambridge, MA: Harvard University Press, 1988.

Morozov, Evgeny. *To Save Everything, Click Here: The Folly of Technological Solutionism*. New York: Public Affairs, 2013.

Neate, Rupert. "Billionaires' Wealth Rises to $10.2 Trillion Amid Covid Crisis." *The Guardian*, October 6, 2020. https://www.theguardian.com/business/2020/oct/07/covid-19-crisis-boosts-the-fortunes-of-worlds-billionaires.

Ng, Joanna. "How Artificial Super-Intelligence Is Today's Tower of Babel." *Christianity Today* (June 17, 2020). https://www.christianitytoday.com/ct/2020/june-web-only/artificial-intelligence-todays-tower-of-babel-ai-ethics.html.

Niebuhr, Reinhold. *Moral Man and Immoral Society*. New York: Scribner's Sons, 1960.

Niebuhr, Richard. *The Nature and Destiny of Man*. 2 vols. New York: Charles Scribner's Sons, 1941–42.

Nietzsche, Friedrich. *The Will to Power*. New York: Penguin Classics, 2017.

O'Collins, Gerald. *Jesus Risen: An Historical, Fundamental and Systematic Examination of Christ's Resurrection*. New York: Paulist, 1987.

———. *What Are They Saying about the Resurrection?* New York: Paulist, 1978.

Paura, Roberto. "A Rapture of the Nerds? A Comparison between Transhumanist Eschatology and Christian Parousia." *Forum Philosophicum* 24.2 (2019) 343–67. DOI:10.35765/forphil.2019.2402.15.

Pearcey, Nancy R. *Love Thy Body.* Grand Rapids: Baker, 2018.

Peters, Ted. "Artificial Intelligence versus Agape Love: Spirituality in a Posthuman Age." *Forum Philosophicum* 24.2 (2019) 259–78. DOI:10.35765/forphil.2019.2402.12.

———. "The Boundaries of Human Nature." *Dialog* 54.1 (2015) 3–7.

———. "Progress and Provolution: Will Transhumanism Leave Sin Behind?" In *Transhumanism and Transcendence: Christian Hope in an Age of Technological Enhancement*, edited by Ronald Cole-Turner, 63–86. Washington, DC: Georgetown University Press, 2011.

———. "Radical Life Extension, Cybernetic Immortality, and Techno-salvation. Really?" *Dialog* 57.4 (December 2018) 250–56. https://doi.org/10.1111/dial.12432.

Peterson-Withorn, Chase. "How Much Money America's Billionaires Have Made during the Covid-19 Pandemic." *Forbes*, April 30, 2021. https://www.forbes.com/sites/chasewithorn/2021/04/30/american-billionaires-have-gotten-12-trillion-richer-during-the-pandemic/?sh=61809fddf557

Prisco, Giulio. "Christianity and Transhumanism Are Much Closer Than You Think." In *Tales of the Turing Church: Hacking Religion, Enlightening Science, Awakening Technology*, by Giulio Prisco, 72–89. 2nd ed. Self published: n.p., 2020.

Prusak, Bernard P. "Bodily Resurrection in Catholic Perspective." *Theological Studies* 61.1 (2000) 64–105.

Rahner, Karl. *On the Theology of Death.* Translated by C. H. Henkey. 1961. Reprint, New York: Herder & Herder, 1972.

———. "The Resurrection of the Body." In *Theological Investigations, Volume 2.* translated by Karl-H Kruger, 2:210–11. 23 vols. Baltimore: Helicon, 1963.

Ramsey, Paul. *Fabricated Man: The Ethics of Genetic Control.* New Haven: Yale University Press, 1970.

Ratzinger, Joseph. *Introduction to Christianity.* Translated by J. R. Foster. New York: Herder & Herder, 1970.

Rothblatt, Martine. *Virtually Human: The Promise and the Peril of Digital Immortality.* New York: Picador, 2014.

Sandberg, Anders, and Nick Bostrom. "Whole Brain Emulation: A Roadmap." Technical Report No 2008-3, Future of Humanity Institute, Oxford University, 2008.

Schopenhauer, Arthur, ed. *Richard Taylor, the Will to Live: Selected Writings.* New York: Ungar, 1967.

Schwab, Klaus. *The Fourth Industrial Revolution.* New York: Penguin, 2017.

Schwab, Klaus, and Thierry Malleret. *COVID-19: The Great Reset.* Geneva: Forum, 2020. http://reparti.free.fr/schwab2020.pdf

Shatzer, Jacob. *Transhumanism and the Image of God.* Downers Grove, IL: InterVarsity, 2019.

Silver, Lee. *Remaking Eden: Cloning and Beyond in a Brave New World*. New York: Avon, 1998.

Simut, Ciprian. "The Doctrine of the Resurrection of the Body in the Theological Thought of Thomas Burnet." *Perichoresis* 18.2 (2020) 31–45. DOI: 10.2478/perc-2020-0009.

Tegmark, Max. *Life 3.0: Being Human in the Age of Artificial Intelligence*. New York: Doubleday, 2017.

Teilhard de Chardin, Pierre. *Science and Christ*. New York: Harper & Row, 1968.

Thweatt-Bates, Jennifer Jeanine. "Artificial Wombs and Cyborg Births: Postgenderism and Theology." In *Transhumanism and Transcendence: Christian Hope in an Age of Technological Enhancement*, edited by Ronald Cole-Turner, 101–14. Washington, DC: Georgetown University Press, 2011.

———. "The Cyborg Christ: Theological Anthropology, Christology, and the Posthuman." (2010) Order No. 3441866, Princeton Theological Seminary.

———. *Cyborg Selves: A Theological Anthropology of the Posthuman*. Farnham, UK: Ashgate, 2012.

Tillich, Paul. *Systematic Theology III*. 3 vols. Chicago: University of Chicago Press, 1963.

Tipler, Frank J. "The Omega Point as Eschaton: Answers to Pannenberg's Questions for Scientists." *Zygon* 24.2 (1989) 217–53.

———. *The Physics of Immortality: Modern Cosmology, God, and the Resurrection of the Dead*. New York: Doubleday, 1994.

Tucker, Ian. "Neuroscientist Dr Hannah Critchlow: Changing the Way That You Think Is Cognitively Costly." *The Guardian* (May 11, 2019). https://www.theguardian.com/science/2019/may/11/neuroscientist-dr-hannah-critchlow-science-of-fate-interview.

Vallor, Shannon. *Technology and the Virtues: A Philosophical Guide to a Future Worth Wanting*. New York: Oxford, 2016.

Vatican Council II. *Gaudium et Spes*. https://www.vatican.va/archive/hist_councils/ii_vatican_council/documents/vat-ii_const_19651207_gaudium-et-spes_en.html.

Vicini, Andrea, and Agnes M. Brazal. "Longing for Transcendence: Cyborgs and Trans- and Posthuman." *Theological Studies* 76.1 (2015) 148–65. DOI: 10.1177/0040563914565308.

Von Neumann, John, and Arthur W. Burks. *Theory of Self-Reproducing Automata*. Urbana: University of Illinois Press, 1966.

Waldstein, Michael. "Introduction." In *Man and Woman He Created Them: A Theology of the Body*, by John Paul II, 1–128. Translated by Michael Waldstein. Boston: Pauline, 2006.

Waters, Brent. "Flesh Made Data: The Posthuman Project in Light of the Incarnation." In *Religion and Transhumanism: The Unknown Future of Human Enhancement*, edited by Calvin Mercer and Tracy Trothen, 291–302. Santa Barbara, CA: Praeger, 2015.

————. "Whose Salvation? Which Eschatology? Transhumanism and Christianity as Contending Salvific Religions." In *Transhumanism and Transcendence: Christian Hope in an Age of Technological Enhancement*, edited by Ronald Cole-Turner, 163–76. Washington, DC: Georgetown University Press, 2011.

Watts, Fraser. "The Multifaceted Nature of Human Personhood: Psychological and Theological Perspectives." In *Questioning the Human: Toward a Theological Anthropology for the Twenty-First Century*, edited by Lieven Boeve et al., 41–63. Fordham University Press, 2014.

Welton, Donn. "Biblical Bodies." In *Body & Flesh: A Philosophical Reader*, edited by Donn Welton, 243–55. Oxford: Blackwell, 1998.

"World Inequality Report 2022." *Reuters.* https://graphics.reuters.com/ GLOBAL-ECONOMY/BILLIONAIRES/klvykndqgvg/wealth-inequalty_wealth.jpg.

Wright, N. T. *Paul and the Faithfulness of God*. London: SPCK, 2013.

————. *The Resurrection of the Son of God: Christian Origins and the Question of God*. Vol 3. 4 vols. London: Fortress, 2003.

Yanez-Fernandez. "David I. Dubrovsky and Merab Mamardashvili: Adam's Second Fall and the Advent of the Cyber-Leviathan." *Forum Philosophicum* 24.2 (2019) 301–41. DOI:10.35765/forphil.2019.2402.14.

Young, George M. *The Russian Cosmists: The Esoteric Futurism of Nikolai Fedorov and His Followers*. Oxford: Oxford University Press, 2012.

Young, Simon. *Designer Evolution: A Transhumanist Manifesto*. Amherst, NY: Prometheus, 2006.

Zuckerberg, Mark. "Connect 2021: Our Vision for the Metaverse." *Facebook* (October 28, 2021). https://www.facebook.com/4/videos/1898414763675286/.

www.ingramcontent.com/pod-product-compliance
Lightning Source LLC
Chambersburg PA
CBHW060423090426
42734CB00011B/2422